ENCOUNTERING
YOUR
ANGELS

BIBLICAL PROOF THAT
ANGELS ARE HERE TO HELP

JOSHUA MILLS

WHITAKER
HOUSE

ENCOUNTERING YOUR ANGELS:
Biblical Proof That Angels Are Here to Help

International Glory Ministries
P.O. Box 4037 • Palm Springs, CA 92263
JoshuaMills.com
info@joshuamills.com

ISBN: 978-1-64123-390-3
eBook ISBN: 978-1-64123-391-0
Printed in the United States of America
© 2020 by Joshua Mills

Whitaker House
1030 Hunt Valley Circle
New Kensington, PA 15068
www.whitakerhouse.com

Library of Congress Control Number: 2020932338

1 2 3 4 5 6 7 8 9 10 11 **WH** 27 26 25 24 23 22 21 20

DEDICATION

This book is dedicated to Jesus and His angels. Thank You for sharing Yourself and for trusting me with the precious things of heaven.

CONTENTS

INTRODUCTION

I first became aware of angels when I was just a young boy. After a while, I stopped seeing them, but when I was in my early twenties, the Lord kindly opened up a new season of my life through a dream and began teaching me, in His own way, about this very important angelic realm.

The realm of angels is amazing because it's a realm of God! You must understand that God created angels, and everything that God creates has significance. As believers, we cannot afford to ignore the angels that God has given to us as co-laborers in the ministry assignments He has ordained for us to complete.

I have written a book called Seeing Angels that I would highly recommend if you want to understand more about angels, especially the scriptural ins and outs of recognizing and interacting with them on a daily basis.

In this book, Encountering Your Angels, we're going to focus on fifty-two actual encounters between angels and humans (both men and women) that are recorded in both the Old and New Testaments. Through these encounters with angels, people received help, encouragement, miracles, deliverance, and so much more.

Although these encounters will take you straight through the Bible, this book is not so much about what has happened in the past as it is about what God wants to do for you, right now. My prayer is that the Scriptures will come alive for you as the living

Word. I believe that God wants to introduce you to these ministering spirits who will work with and for you today to help accomplish His purposes in your life. Angels are sent to help you recover from yesterday's setbacks, overcome today's challenges, and win tomorrow's battles.

Some people question the validity of angelic ministry for today, assuming that their services are no longer needed now that we have received the promised gift of the Holy Spirit. But scripturally, that kind of thinking is incorrect. The early church not only embraced the idea of God's angels as helpers in our lives, but according to Scripture, it's obvious that they were also very familiar with their actual day-to-day ministry. For example, about fourteen years after Jesus ascended into heaven and sent us His Spirit, an angel brought deliverance to Peter, who was awaiting his death sentence in a jail cell. Later, when he arrived at the home where the believers had been praying for him, they couldn't believe it was really Peter, insisting, *"It must be his angel"* (Acts 12:15 NIV). Clearly, those early followers of Christ knew about the angels that are assigned to the lives of faith-filled believers.

Also consider the truth that there are more angelic encounters in the New Testament than in the Old Testament. I believe that's a sign that as we get closer to the return of Christ, angelic activity will be much more prevalent upon the earth.

Today, the Holy Spirit is illuminating this topic of study once again. Not only are we coming to know about God's angels, but we are also able to recognize, experience, and appreciate the truth that they've been sent to help us every single day of our lives. I firmly believe that every angel encounter documented within the pages of your Bible represents an area of need in your life for which God has angels available to assist you too! And that's why I've collected these accounts for you. I want you to see it in the Word, I want you to grasp it by faith, and I want you to take hold of it for your own life.

God's Word tells us that these angels are *"ministering spirits, sent forth to minister for them who shall be heirs of salvation"* (Hebrews 1:14) If you have invited Jesus Christ to be Lord over your life, then He has angels that He wants to introduce to you—angels who will help you, guide you, protect you, comfort you, bring healing to you, strengthen you, and lead you into living a more vibrant life, fully committed to God's purposes.

I invite you to dive into this book and begin *Encountering Your Angels.*

A PROPHETIC WORD FROM JERUSALEM

On the first morning of Sukkot (or Feast of the Tabernacles), while I was in Israel ministering at the Pontifical Institute Notre Dame of Jerusalem Center, the Spirit began to speak a prophetic word through me that I believe was not only significant for the gathering of people in that place but also for you right now—even as you prepare to read this book. This prophecy is being released from Mount Zion to the ends of the earth, and it deals with the increase of angelic involvement that God desires to bring into the lives of His people in order for His purposes to be accomplished. Prayers and decrees are important, but just as important is our willingness to discern the movement of God's ministering Spirits when they come. Read this prophetic word aloud and decree it over your life as you prepare to begin encountering your angels:

> The Lord says, "I am releasing and dispatching My angels over your life right now. Some of you have been praying and praying and praying, but you must know that I have heard your prayers. They have not fallen on deaf ears, for I AM the Lord that hears you. I have heard My Word on the lips of My people and I am responding to your prayers in this day. And even right now, during this season of My glory-covering, angels with supernatural abundance are being assigned upon the prayers that you have prayed. In the same way that I sent an angel to Daniel after he prayed, and I sent an angel to visit Cornelius after he prayed, and I sent my angel to deliver Peter when

the early church prayed, and I sent an angel to minister strength to Jesus while He prayed in the garden, so I AM sending angels to you now in response to your prayers. There are angels of deliverance that are being released into the middle of your situation. Angels of healing are coming now to minister to areas of need. Many angels are being released, for I have commanded My angels concerning you, and they shall work with those who are open and ready to work with them.

"In the days ahead, you must discern what I am doing and how I am moving so that you may open up the door to let My angels flow into your life with miracles. Open your spirit-eyes to see. Open your spirit-ears to hear. Open your spiritual senses and fully and prepare to see My Spirit moving in your midst in a new way. Angels are being dispatched for My purposes. Spirit winds are beginning to blow once again, and you may even feel the brush of their wings. Wingtip to wingtip, they are gathering all around you. I am sheltering you within My divine protection as My angels are hovering over you. Breakthrough is being loosed upon you. Prepare to receive the answers to your intercession as My heavenly host are dispatched into your areas of need.

"O yes, in areas where you've struggled for a long time, the Lord says, "There shall be no more struggle as you find yourself coming into a rest and an ease of My Presence, which you have not known in days gone by. O yes, there shall be a new rest that shall overtake your spirit, your soul, and even your physical well-being. You shall enter into a new ease of My Presence and a new ease of My glory—where My Word is your lamp and your voice decrees loose that light. You shall see miracles, miracles, miracles. Some miracles that you've been praying for are right around the corner, but coming with them are a multiplication of miracles that you haven't even asked for—but I am sending them in this day," says the Lord.

"For My goodness shall overwhelm you, and My glory shall overtake you for My purposes to be fulfilled in your life. As you lift Me up, so shall I lift you up, and I will do it through the ministry service of My angels," says the Lord.

Prophetic word given to Joshua Mills
Jerusalem, Israel

1

ANGELS TO THE RESCUE

An angel rescued and comforted Hagar.

The angel of the LORD found Hagar near a spring in the desert; it was the spring that is beside the road to Shur. And he said, "Hagar, slave of Sarai, where have you come from, and where are you going?" "I'm running away from my mistress Sarai," she answered. Then the angel of the LORD told her, "Go back to your mistress and submit to her." The angel added, "I will increase your descendants so much that they will be too numerous to count."   (Genesis 16:7–10 NIV)

Have you ever felt betrayed and discouraged? This must've been how Hagar felt before the angel appeared to her near the spring in the desert. This angel came to rescue Hagar by speaking God's blessings over her life.

Angels deliver messages—they are God's messengers. They do not originate the messages, but they deliver them faithfully and resourcefully, communicating with the intended recipient in countless ways that always meet the person—in this case, a run-away servant girl named Hagar, right where she was. Hagar did not ask for an angelic visitation. She had run off into the desert with her son (fathered by Sarai's husband, Isaac) because she could not tolerate her mistress's abuse any longer. She was angry and afraid. But God wanted her to know that He had a plan for her life. His message was, "I don't want you to die out here in the desert. Go back to your mistress and be obedient. Eventually, through this child of yours, you will have countless descendants." Hagar obeyed the message.

Several years ago, we had the privilege of meeting a young girl named Victoria. Her grandparents had driven her all the way from Florida (where they lived) so she could visit us as we were hosting a week-long Glory Conference in Canada. When Victoria was four years old, she experienced something supernatural. One afternoon, she was playing around her swimming pool, but when she went to go down the waterslide, she accidentally fell from the top—a nine-foot drop. Instead of being seriously injured or experiencing any pain, however, she reported that in that moment, six large angels swooped her up into their arms and gently placed her little body onto the concrete patio below. Her grandparents, who witnessed the entire experience, testified to us that her story was true! It is unexplainable in the natural that her body was uninjured, but we serve a God who cares about every little detail of our lives, and His angels are ready to come and rescue us when danger looms near. This testimony became a great encouragement to many people around the world.

Not too long ago, I read a story about another four-year-old child named Patrick. He had been on vacation with his family at a resort in Hawaii when, without them knowing, he wandered off by himself, fell into the deep end of the pool, and drowned. A nurse who was lounging in the hot tub noticed Patrick's lifeless body floating in the pool and immediately rushed to his side to begin performing CPR. Thankfully, Patrick's precious life was saved. Later, when Patrick was questioned about what happened, he recalled being face down on the bottom of the pool, unable to breathe at all. Then, he said, "two huge ladies with wings" picked him up off the bottom of the pool, flipped him face up, and lifted him to the water's surface. Patrick's parents believed what he said because each morning, they had prayed protection through the blood of Jesus over each of their children, then, each night when tucking them into bed, they also prayed with their children and always thanked God for the angels who encamped around them. Now, the reality of those prayers had come to pass and saved their child's life.

It is important to remind not only ourselves but also our children that God's angels are ready and willing to help whenever we ask.

ANGEL PRAYER

Heavenly Father, as my loving heavenly Father, I know You wish to rescue and encourage me and all of Your children as we endeavor to walk the narrow way of faith. (See Matthew 7:13.) Often, Your strengthening words come directly from Your written Word, and at other times, they come from fellow believers. But—especially when I am alone and in need—please be quick to send me an angelic messenger to lift me up and set my feet on the right path again. In joyful anticipation, I thank You. In Jesus's name, amen.

2

ANGELS BRING DIVINE PROVISION

An angel helped Hagar and her son.

> *And God heard the voice of the lad; and the angel of God called to Hagar out of heaven, and said unto her, What aileth thee, Hagar? fear not; for God hath heard the voice of the lad where he is. Arise, lift up the lad, and hold him in thine hand; for I will make him a great nation. And God opened her eyes, and she saw a well of water; and she went, and filled the bottle with water, and gave the lad drink.* (Genesis 21:17–19 KJV)

We don't know the age of Hagar's son at this time, but he was young enough for her to carry him in her arms. It appears that he had been crying because he was so hot and thirsty. Why was his mother doing this? She had rushed out of the tent in such a hurry, so upset, and she didn't seem to care if they both died. It's hard to survive very long in the desert without supplies.

God's angel had to intervene. Speaking to Hagar by name (which is notable, too, because it shows us that God and His angels actually know who we are) the angel not only predicted a long-term blessing for Hagar's young son, Ishmael, but he also supplied the most urgent need first—drinking water. That's real help, right on time.

No personal need is too small—or too large. Years ago, my wife and I had to leave suddenly on a ministry trip to Indonesia without adequate time to pack for ourselves and our young son.

It was Christmas Day and we had to leave behind a messy house, which was going to be difficult to return to in January.

But when we got home and walked in the door, we were stunned to see that the house was spotless and the Christmas decorations had been put away exactly as we would have done. What a wonderful gift! I guessed that my mother must have come over, so I called to thank her. No, she said she hadn't had time. "Well, who could have done it?" I asked, and we had no answer.

Could the Lord have sent an angelic cleaning crew to our home? We know He cares about every detail of our lives, and He knows what is important to us. Only He could have demonstrated such a meticulous concern for meeting our needs, down to knowing exactly how to store the Christmas decorations. The longer we thought about it, the more sure we became that God had sent "cleaning angels" to take care of our mess. What a gift!

ANGEL PRAYER

Heavenly Father, please take care of me when I am so needy that I cannot even formulate the words of a coherent prayer. Please receive my wordless cries as prayer requests and supply what I lack. Even when I do not know what I need, send help. Even when it is not a matter of life and death, please send an angel of mercy to provide exactly what is called for, before it's too late. Oh, thank You, dear Lord, for Your fatherly concern for my every need, spoken or unspoken. In Jesus's name, amen.

3

MEN OR ANGELS?

Three angels visited Abraham in his tent.

> *And he lifted up his eyes and looked, and, lo, three men stood by him: and when he saw them, he ran to meet them from the tent door, and bowed himself toward the ground.*
>
> (Genesis 18:2)

At first, Abraham thought that his visitors were three ordinary, travel-weary men, and he jumped up to show them some Eastern hospitality. He gave them water for washing their feet and ordered his servant to prepare the finest calf from the herd, to be served with curds and milk.

Only after they had eaten did Abraham begin to suspect that they were angelic visitors. When they asked for his elderly wife Sarah by name and then predicted that she would become pregnant within the year, even though she laughed at the very thought, their prophecy came true.

It's a good thing Abraham gave them such a warm welcome. Those three "men" turned out to be angels in human disguise! This is why the writer of Hebrews instructs us: *"Do not forget to show hospitality to strangers, for by so doing some people have shown hospitality to angels without knowing it"* (Hebrews 13:2 NIV).

Angels can assume the appearance of either men or women of any size, as well as other physical forms, such as animals. (See Zechariah 1:8–11, 5:9; 2 Kings 2:11–12, 6:13–17; Ezekiel 1, 10.) They can also appear in spiritual dimensions such as visions, trances, and dreams.

Recently, I had the opportunity to be interviewed by Bob Dutko for his daily radio talk show on WMUZ, the most-listened-to Christian radio station in Detroit, Michigan. During our conversation, I mentioned to Bob that angels often appear to us in ways that we don't initially recognize. He agreed and related a special story to me about something that happened to him several years prior. While attending a funeral service, the minister on duty gave an altar call for people to receive salvation (which was the desire of the deceased). After the service concluded, several family members and friends of the deceased made ugly comments about the minister's proselytizing during the funeral. Bob sat with the downcast minister at a table during the luncheon that followed. At the end of the meal, Bob noticed that the minister's countenance had changed. When Bob asked about it, the man told him that he had received encouragement from the distinguished man with the blue jacket and white hair. But who was this man? Bob hadn't seen him. The astonished minister said, "He was right here. You didn't see him?" Bob looked around the room, even went outside to check the parking lot, and still, there was no sign of a man with a blue jacket and white hair. Both men came to the same conclusion: it must have been an angel sent to bring the minster encouragement. Bob told me, "I still feel goosebumps when I talk about it today."

I recently heard a story from a friend who had experienced the horrendous aftermath of Hurricane Harvey, which caused great flooding in Houston, Texas, in 2017. On that first night, when the power was out and everything was pitch black, he was attempting to walk home to save his wife's musical instruments. In the darkness, he accidentally stumbled into the bayou. Once he managed to get himself back onto the grass, he suddenly saw a stranger wearing a black garbage bag. With nobody else in sight, he asked the stranger, "Why are you out here?" The man told my friend that he was "on the night shift." This stranger led my friend to a place where he was able to continue the journey safely on his own. It later occurred to him that this unusual encounter could've been an angel on secret assignment. When I heard this story, I was reminded of the Bible verse that says, *"When you go through deep waters, I will be with you. When you go through rivers of difficulty, you will not drown"* (Isaiah 43:2 NLT).

Angels seem to appear as ordinary humans (in whatever context) when they need to work with people in a practical way to accomplish a clear objective. Seldom do we recognize them as angels until they have departed.

Once, I asked the Lord why He does it this way. In my spirit, I felt Him respond, "Joshua, on most occasions, identifying them as angels would distract from the purpose for which I sent them. However, if it brings peace and comfort to My children, I will allow them to be recognized."

ANGEL PRAYER

Heavenly Father, as You eventually opened Abraham's eyes to see the three strangers as angels, grant me discerning eyes to see the angels around me who appear to be ordinary people, dressed in unremarkable ways and speaking my language. By helping me to see them, I pray that You will emphasize to me the importance of the messages they bring. Surely I will be quicker to worship You when I realize what has just transpired. Thank You for sending angelic helpers to me so that I can follow You more closely. I pray in Jesus's name, amen.

4

THE ANGEL OF THE LORD

An angel provided a ram for Abraham's sacrifice.

And the angel of the LORD called unto him out of heaven, and said, Abraham, Abraham: and he said, Here am I. And he said, Lay not thine hand upon the lad, neither do thou any thing unto him: for now I know that thou fearest God, seeing thou hast not withheld thy son, thine only son from me. And Abraham lifted up his eyes, and looked, and behold behind him a ram caught in a thicket by his horns: and Abraham went and took the ram, and offered him up for a burnt offering in the stead of his son. And Abraham called the name of that place Jehovahjireh: as it is said to this day, In the mount of the LORD *it shall be seen. And the angel of the* LORD *called unto Abraham out of heaven the second time, and said, By myself have I sworn, saith the* LORD, *for because thou hast done this thing, and hast not withheld thy son, thine only son: that in blessing I will bless thee, and in multiplying I will multiply thy seed as the stars of the heaven, and as the sand which is upon the sea shore; and thy seed shall possess the gate of his enemies; and in thy seed shall all the nations of the earth be blessed; because thou hast obeyed my voice.* (Genesis 22:11–18 KJV)

Is the *"angel of the* LORD*"* one of God's created angelic beings, or God Himself, appearing in human form? We cannot be absolutely sure, although most students of the Bible lean toward the latter conclusion. God's promise is: *"The angel of the* LORD *encamps around those who fear him, and he delivers them"* (Psalm 34:7 NIV).

The *"angel of the* LORD*."* It seems that whenever this phrasing appears, an especially vital message needs to be delivered or an important action needs to be performed. A good example is when the angel of the Lord told Joseph about the birth of Jesus: *"But while he thought on these things, behold, the angel of the Lord appeared to him in a dream, saying, Joseph, you son of David, fear not to take to you Mary your wife: for that which is conceived in her is of the Holy Ghost. And she shall bring forth a son, and you shall call His name* JESUS: *for He shall save His people from their sins"* (Matthew 1:20–21).

Also in the New Testament, we see the angel of the Lord helping Peter to escape from prison (see Acts 12:7) and then striking down the evil King Herod (see Acts 12:23). In any case, God Himself has initiated the actions. And—wonderful to think about—the same angel of the Lord who moved and ministered in ancient times is still ready to minister on our behalf today.

We love to visit a beautiful oasis near our ministry base in Palm Springs, California. An angel seems to stand guard over that place, stationed at a waterfall and usually wearing a rainbow halo or a rainbow belt. We have had many angelic encounters in that place and, occasionally, we lead groups of people on a special hike along the mile-long path back to this "open portal." During our most recent encounter, some people noticed a double rainbow, which spoke of God's covenant and double-blessing promises. And yet, most people, although they could feel angels at the oasis, could not see any. As we worshipped for a while, suddenly our eyes were opened to see seven rams standing on the mountain. These bighorn sheep were clearly signs of God's promises and blessings, since seven is God's number. Just as God sent the provisional ram to Abraham, we believe that He will provide for us today. We felt that angels of provision were actively displacing lack, insufficiency, and suffering—and we rejoiced.

Several days later, the testimonies began to come in from those who were present. An unemployed woman had been offered an office position better than she had hoped for. Another lady was supernaturally blessed so that she could make a much-desired cross-country move. Another family reported an influx of financial provisions and unusual opportunities. These are some of the things we should expect to happen when God's angels show up!

ANGEL PRAYER

Heavenly Father, when I encounter an angel, I am not asking to know the difference between an "ordinary" one and when You Yourself are choosing to appear as an angel. You are the sovereign Initiator of all such encounters, and You are the only One I worship. However, I do ask that you will keep my heart tender and my will pliant so that I will be able to cooperate obediently with everything You desire. In Jesus's everlasting name, amen.

5

MINISTERING SPIRITS

Lot showed hospitality to two visiting angels.

And there came two angels to Sodom at even; and Lot sat in the gate of Sodom: and Lot seeing them rose up to meet them; and he bowed himself with his face toward the ground; and he said, Behold now, my lords, turn in, I pray you, into your servant's house, and tarry all night, and wash your feet, and ye shall rise up early, and go on your ways. And they said, Nay;

but we will abide in the street all night. And he pressed upon them greatly; and they turned in unto him, and entered into his house; and he made them a feast, and did bake unleavened bread, and they did eat.   (Genesis 19:1–3 KJV)

Lot could not be blamed for thinking that the two angels were, in fact, travelers to whom he should show hospitality. Evidently, they were dressed in typical garments and looked like ordinary men. They could eat food because they partook of the feast he prepared. (Angels can choose to eat or not, as necessary, and they will adopt local styles and customs to suit the need at hand.)

These angels are known as "ministering spirits." *"Are [angels] not all ministering spirits, sent forth to minister for them who shall be heirs of salvation?"* (Hebrews 1:14). They are the kinds of angels we interact with the most, abiding within the first heaven (the earthly realm), and carry out God's many orders among His people. These angels provide protection, support, deliverance, miracles, and healing. According to the Scriptures, they have been commissioned to our lives by God as heavenly messengers, and their success requires our cooperation, which, as it turned out, was somewhat difficult to obtain from Lot!

As I was preparing this book, I received this testimony from overseas, sent by an editor who was translating my book, *Seeing Angels*. In her email, she wrote: "I live in Indonesia; I'm a translator and editor for two publishers. Right now, I'm translating Joshua Mills's book *Seeing Angels*, and I'm about 60 percent finishing it…. I'm so excited about the teaching and revelations. So far, I follow every instructions in the book, including the prayers—and it works! Two days ago, after working on that book until 2:45 a.m.,

I prayed, then I went to bed. But I could not sleep yet, because of the sadness which was still bothering me. (My mom just passed away last month, and at the same time, my boyfriend turned away from me because of being scared of a committed relationship....) Around 3:00 a.m., I lie down on my left side, still wide awake, far from sleepy. Suddenly, I felt a hand tapped my right upper arm two times. I quickly turned my head to see who did it. (I was alone in my room.) Sure enough, I did not see anybody.... My spirit could feel that it was not from any evil spirit, because I felt a peaceful presence. I asked God in my heart, 'God, was it one of my angels?' In my spirit, I felt a confirmation that it was my angel who did it. ... Even just translating Joshua's book is helping me to have a 'warming-up encounter' with one of my angels, and I cannot wait for other encounters to come. Praise God!"

I am convinced that any believer can learn to recognize and interact with his or her angels as we see what Scripture tells us and learn to open our hearts and spirits to the supernatural realm.

ANGEL PRAYER

Heavenly Father, I thank You for angel encounters in my city, my home, my workplace, and everywhere I go. I thank You for encompassing my life with Your angels of protection, deliverance, and comfort. I can feel their guarding presence around me and I ask You to open the eyes of my heart to see them at work. I trust that Your angels of deliverance and abundant provision are working here and now to bring blessing into my life. In Jesus's strong name, amen.

6

DREAM MESSENGERS

Jacob saw angels ascending and descending a ladder.

He had a dream in which he saw a stairway resting on the earth, with its top reaching to heaven, and the angels of God were ascending and descending on it. (Genesis 28:12 NIV)

Jacob was on a journey, sleeping outdoors and using a rock as a pillow, when he saw a number of angels in his dream. They were going up and down a ladder that reached into heaven. When he woke up, he was sure that the dream portrayed reality—so sure that he dedicated his stone pillow to mark the spot as *"the gate of heaven"* (Genesis 28:17)

Later, Joseph, Mary's husband, had at least three dreams in which an angel told him what to do regarding the baby Jesus. In the first dream, he was told to go ahead and take the pregnant Mary as his wife. (See Matthew 1:20–21.) In the second dream, he was warned to move his small family to faraway Egypt because King Herod was on a rampage and the child would be in danger. (See Matthew 2:13.) In the third dream, the angel gave him the "all clear" to return from Egypt to Israel. (See Matthew 2:19–20.) All of these angel visitations took dream form, and Joseph obeyed the angel's message each time.

My own initial connection with my guardian angels took place through a dream. I was not awake when I encountered them. The fact that my encounter took place in the context of a dream does not diminish its validity in the least. Angelic messages, if responded to in faithful obedience, are no less powerful when they come through dreams.

My friend Andrew encountered an angel during the night who actually helped him to patent an invention. During a twenty-one-day fast, he suddenly felt a heavenly presence enter his bedroom. There was such a powerful presence of God's glory radiating from the angel that all Andrew could do was keep perfectly still in his bed because he recognized that something was about to happen. Then, Andrew heard two loud sounds—"thunk, thunk." The pages of the large family Bible began turning, seemingly all on their own. Could it have been a breeze or a wind blowing through the room? No, all the windows were shut. It seemed as though an angel was physically interacting with a natural object in the room. The pages of that large Bible turned all the way from the New Testament, where Andrew had been reading, to the beginning of the Old Testament, where Andrew decided he would begin reading. Over the course of three days, Andrew continued to contemplate the connection between the verse he had read in the book of Matthew and the new verse in Exodus that had been presented to him by an angel. Suddenly, the connection became obvious. It had to do with a business solution that he needed! Through this angelic encounter, Andrew was given the business plan, product design, and patent guidance for this new invention.

Be open to God-sent, angelic dreams and nighttime encounters. Such an experience may be exactly what you need.

ANGEL PRAYER

Heavenly Father, I need Your wise advice and guidance. I pray that You will speak to me in the best ways, including through my dreams while I sleep. Don't let me forget about the "dream option." Create an expectancy in me to hear Your words through Your angelic messengers, and to recognize such words as coming from You—even when they come to me as I sleep. Thank you! I pray this in Jesus's name, amen.

7

ANGELS HELP TO BRING SOLUTIONS

An angel spoke to Jacob in a dream, telling him to return to his homeland

And the angel of God spoke to me in a dream, saying, Jacob: and I said, Here am I. And He said, ...Now arise, get you out from this land, and return to the land of thy kindred.

(Genesis 31:11–13)

Jacob believed the message the angel of God spoke to him in a dream, and he obeyed the instructions. He recognized God's wisdom given to him through the angels and he received it as given within the context of his dreams. Jacob did not discount the angelic injunction as "just a dream," and neither should we, although we should ask the Lord for further confirmation of drastic actions. He will be sure to give it.

When an angel appears to you in a dream and offers you a solution to a problem you face, or when an angel brings you advice about something you have not been able to resolve, you will notice that you will feel much more peaceful and secure when you wake up. Now you have a clear direction and you can proceed on the right path.

In Hawaii, about a decade ago, I had a powerful encounter with angels while I was sleeping. I dreamed that angels were pouring oil into a number of brightly colored boxes—vivid colors like red, orange, green, blue, yellow—and in those boxes, I could see groups of people. I knew in my spirit that each box represented a church. In one box, the people would be gathered somberly; in the next one, the people would be worshipping with hands upraised. The angels were pouring oil onto the people in the boxes regardless of whether they were worshipping or not, but the boxes with worshipers got filled to the brim first, and when they were filled, they sort of melted—box, oil, people—into a flow of oil that was colored the same as the box. The angels would go back to pour more oil on the people who were resisting and each time, they would open up a little bit more. The angels went back, again and again, until each box filled and dissolved.

The colored streams of oil swirled together and went down into the earth. As the oil seeped down, I could see against it the blackness of the sin of the island of Oahu—drug-dealing, prostitution, and more. When all of the boxes were gone, the streaming oil just sort of shot up through all the blackness, like a gusher, removing the sin on one island of Hawaii after another.

When I woke up from the dream, actual oil was flowing from my hands. I let the oil flow for forty-five minutes to an hour, and collected about a quarter-cup of it. This experience was a powerful prophetic message for the whole of Hawaii.

God is sending His angelic hosts to help us in our most difficult situations. In my dream, I believe they were helping believers receive the anointing of the Holy Spirit—until it overflowed—which, in turn, allowed breakthrough to come.

ANGEL PRAYER

Heavenly Father, hear me when I say that I am hungry for more. As I obey You and follow Your Holy Spirit, I want to experience anything You intend for me. Position me to see angels, and help me to begin to comprehend the messages they are bringing from You. Clear my way of distractions and deceptions and help me pay attention with my spirit. I welcome all divine dreams and holy encounters, and I declare my intention to cooperate with Your initiatives. In Jesus's wonderful name, amen.

8

SEE GOD'S GLORY ALL AROUND YOU

Angels accompanied Jacob on his trip home.

> *And Jacob went on his way, and the angels of God met him. And when Jacob saw them, he said, This is God's host: and he called the name of that place Mahanaim [that is, two hosts or camps].*   (Genesis 32:1–2)

To see into God's realms of glory, you don't have to be a Jacob (the patriarch) or a John (the beloved disciple who wrote about his visit to heaven in the book of Revelation). The colonial preacher Jonathan Edwards once said, "The seeking of the kingdom of God is the chief business of the Christian life." It's a given for every believer.

God wants you to seek His kingdom here, on earth. And without a doubt, that includes seeing His angels. He has given you gifts of the Spirit, including the gift of discerning of spirits (see 1 Corinthians 12:10), so that you can explore His glory realms.

In my book, *Moving in Glory Realms*, I wrote about what had happened not long ago when I was ministering in Pensacola, Florida. On the second night of meetings, the cloud of glory that had filled the room visibly increased and expanded. Even those watching online could see it. Miracles started happening all over the room, including physical healings and other signs of God's glory. While I continued to minister, a large, golden handprint appeared on the back of my suit jacket! I am convinced that it was the handprint of the miracle angel that travels with me when I minister. There have been times when others have seen the visible footprints of angels; they looked like a sparkling trail of glory across the carpet at the altar of a church.

A pastor in the Arctic told me that she once saw her congregation filled with angels. All of the people had angels standing directly beside them with their hands on the shoulders of each one. These were angels of love—ministering God's love to each and every one of them.

Always remember that you are pursuing God's glory, not the identifiable evidences of it, such as His angels. You must lean entirely upon the Lord Jesus Christ, the Great Shepherd who has promised to lead you in paths of righteousness. All discernment must flow from your personal relationship with your Savior. But angels are with you!

ANGEL PRAYER

Heavenly Father, You command armies of angels of glorious brightness, all of whom give You praise. Therefore, when I ask You to help me perceive the movements of Your angels around me, I desire to see them so that I can give You even more glory, honor, and praise. I want to live in a revelation of an open heaven every day of my life so that I can praise You with my whole being. Jesus made it possible! In His name I pray, amen.

9

THE SPIRIT OF THE LORD

An angel appeared to Moses in a flame of fire.

*And the angel of the L*ORD *appeared to him in a flame of fire out of the midst of a bush: and he looked, and, behold, the bush burned with fire, and the bush was not consumed.*

(Exodus 3:2)

Once again, here is *"the angel of the LORD"* with a message of vital importance for the plan of God. Biblical scholars have made the connection between the term *"angel of the LORD"* and God or Jesus Himself, appearing in Spirit form. They call it *theophany*—an appearance of the pre-incarnate Christ. This idea is supported by other Old Testament Scriptures in which people react to the angel of the Lord as if he were God Himself, more than an ordinary angel. (Besides this passage, see Exodus 23:21; Genesis 18:25; and Joshua 5:14–15.)

This account states outright that it was God who spoke to Moses out of the bush, saying,

> *Moses! Moses! ...Do not come any closer.... Take off your sandals, for the place where you are standing is holy ground. ...I am the God of your father, the God of Abraham, the God of Isaac and the God of Jacob. ...I have indeed seen the misery of my people in Egypt. I have heard them crying out because of their slave drivers, and I am concerned about their suffering. So I have come down to rescue them from the hand of the Egyptians and to bring them up out of that land into a good and spacious land, a land flowing with milk and honey—the home of the Canaanites, Hittites, Amorites, Perizzites, Hivites and Jebusites. And now the cry of the Israelites has reached me, and I have seen the way the Egyptians are oppressing them. So now, go. I am sending you to Pharaoh to bring my people the Israelites out of Egypt.*
>
> (Exodus 3:4–10 NIV)

Moses couldn't fathom it. How could he bring the Israelites out of Egypt? He negotiated with the Voice coming out of the flames. The Lord, understanding Moses's hesitation, made provision for it, explaining everything. (See Exodus 3:11–21.)

To call God Himself *"the angel of the Lord"* is not meant to imply that He is another angel. He is higher than the angels (see Hebrews 1:4), the only Son of God (see Hebrews 1:1–5), and the One the angels worship (see Hebrews 1:6–7). But angels are spirit beings; thus *"the angel of the Lord"* is the equivalent of "the Spirit of the Lord."

ANGEL PRAYER

Heavenly Father, I fully understand that You Yourself are not a created being like an angel, but I appreciate the fact that You will appear, from time to time, in angelic guise, delivering important messages Yourself. This shows me that You desire to communicate directly with ordinary people like me. Followers of other religions must memorize divine policies and follow them on their own strength, but Your followers need only to listen to Your voice. I worship you! In the name of Your Son, Jesus, amen.

10

GUIDING ANGELS

An angel guided Joshua into battle in the Promised Land.

Behold, I send an angel before you, to keep you in the way, and to bring you into the place which I have prepared. Beware of Him, and obey His voice, provoke Him not; for He will not pardon your transgressions: for My name is in Him. But if you shall indeed obey his voice, and do all that I speak; then I will be an enemy to your enemies, and an adversary to your adversaries. For My angel shall go before you, and bring you in to the Amorites, and the Hittites, and the Perizzites, and the Canaanites, and the Hivites, and the Jebusites: and I will cut them off. (Exodus 23:20–23)

God used an angel to guide Joshua, step by step and battle by battle, into the Promised Land. In subsequent verses, we can read God's extensive instructions and warnings, followed by the actual outworking of God's plan.

Have you ever sensed that your angels were trying to say something to you? I have noticed that most of such communications occur late at night or early in the morning, especially when you are in a position of rest. But they can happen at any time, and sometimes they do not involve words as much as circumstantial arrangements. The common denominator is that all of God's communications are "spirit and life." (See John 6:63.) Increasingly, our spirits learn to trust the flow of new thoughts, ideas, suggestions, or changes that constitute an angel's messages from God.

Our Creator, God, is endlessly creative with His communications. My experience with angels is more extensive than most people's, and yet He continues to surprise me.

I believe that one of the ways our angels can reach out to us, is by getting our attention through numbers and numerical repetitions. A few years ago, as I traveled to minister in Stuttgart, Germany, I kept sensing in my spirit that the Lord wanted me to speak on the topic of the Holy Spirit's anointing. I tossed it around in my spirit during the long ten-hour flight, and I kept being reminded of Jesus's words in Luke 4:18: "*the Spirit of the Lord is upon Me, because He has anointed Me….*" After I finally landed in Frankfurt, I picked up my rental car and drove to Stuttgart with only a couple of hours to spare before my first session began. But when I checked into my hotel, the most supernatural thing happened. The front desk attendant told me that I was in room 418! Most people might not make the connection, but I've trained myself to be aware of the way the Spirit speaks. This wasn't a coincidence; it was a clear sign to me, confirming what God had spoken to my spirit about Luke 4:18.

You see, the angels have a way of clearing paths and arranging things to help you understand God's perfect will. I've noticed that they like to do this with numbers! When you see a sequence of numbers in order or a particular number on repeat—for example, 1234, 1111, 2222, etc.—it is oftentimes an angelic reminder to you that God is bringing things into divine alignment.

Here are a few repeat number sets that I see on a continual basis, constantly reminding me of God's guiding angels and His personal promises over my life as found within Scripture:

111 – God is increasing your blessings in an exponential way. (See Deuteronomy 1:11.)

1111 – You are crossing over into your promised inheritance. (See Deuteronomy 11:11.)

222 – God will confirm His Word to you through faith, action and miracles. (See Acts 2:22; James 2:22.)

2222 – You are being given new keys to new opportunities. (See Isaiah 22:22.)

333 – Hold on…God's promises are coming to pass in your life. (See John 3:33.)

444 – Things are flourishing according to the Word of God. (See Deuteronomy 4:44; 2 Kings 4:44; Isaiah 44:4; Psalm 44:4.)

555 – Great grace and favor are upon you. (See Isaiah 55:5.)

777 – Supernatural doors are being opened to you. (See Matthew 7:7.)

818 – Your life is a sign and wonder for God's glory. (See Isaiah 8:18.)

Isn't it wonderful that angels can remind us of God's Word through numbers? Keep your eyes open and you might begin to see these special messages too!

ANGEL PRAYER

Father God, You are our loving Creator and Shepherd. You surround me with just the right kinds of guidance and protection. I am eager to know what You have in store for me, but I am grateful for the perfect ways in which You send Your communications. Keep me attentive and responsive to Your angels of guidance, I ask in the name of Jesus. Amen.

11

ANGELIC ESCORT

The angel continued to lead Moses despite the people's sin.

> *Therefore now go, lead the people to the place of which I have spoken to you: behold, My angel shall go before you: nevertheless in the day when I visit I will visit their sin upon them.*
>
> (Exodus 32:34)

While Moses was on the mountaintop receiving the tablets of the Ten Commandments, his brother Aaron encouraged the people to create an idol in the form of a calf made of gold. When

Moses found out, he became so infuriated that he threw down the sacred tablets and shattered them. He also burned the golden calf, ground the ashes to powder, and had some of the people slaughtered. These were God's people, the ones he had risked his life for, and they were running wild. He would not have been surprised if the entire Exodus venture would fail utterly as a result.

Seeking the Lord fervently, Moses would have preferred to die himself than to have God abandon them because of their sin. But God spoke to him directly and promised an angelic escort all the way to the Promised Land. Sin would be punished, but God's purposes would be accomplished.

Can you see yourself in this story? Would you follow the crowd blindly and suffer the consequences, or would you admit your sin and get back on board with God's plan? All of us are tempted at some point to worship a false idol of human manufacture. And yet, we belong to a God who is absolutely faithful.

I have a friend who sees bluish-purple sparkles around people's heads. This is the way he recognizes angels. There is no fear in this experience, just unusual activity in the atmosphere. There are many different ways in which your angels can appear; it's given to us to discern their activity and then pray into the situation to understand what God is revealing. Sometimes you will see the activity of angels even though you don't see the actual angel himself, and that's okay too. We know that God's greatest concern toward humanity is for our eternal salvation, so He sends angels to work with us in this regard. Matthew 13:39 tells us that *"the reapers* [harvesters] *are the angels."*

Whether our unfavorable circumstances represent a natural wilderness or come from our own rebellion, God's angels will continue to do His bidding on our behalf. All we need to do is to turn our faces in His direction.

ANGEL PRAYER

Heavenly Father, I am asking You to show me my own sin—my own false idols—so that I can repent and resume my journey of following You to the Promised Land. I do not trust myself to do the right thing. I plead for Your mercy and grace, and I ask for an angelic escort as well. My heart can rest secure as long as I know You will continue to show me the way to go. This is my sincerest plea. In Jesus's name, amen.

12

COMMANDER IN CHIEF

The captain of the angelic host prepared Joshua to take Jericho.

The captain of the LORD's host said to Joshua, Loose your shoe from off your foot; for the place whereon you stand is holy. And Joshua did so.   (Joshua 5:15)

God's angels are often referred to as the "heavenly host," or "mighty ones." They are like a mighty army. And who is the commander of this army? The Lord God Himself. In Scripture, we find one of the names of God is *"Sabaoth"* (Strong's #4519), which literally means "the God of angel armies." (See 1 Samuel 1:3; 15:2; 17:45.) When we call upon that name, He is ready to defend us and send heavenly hosts to war on our behalf.

Here He stands, face-to-face with Joshua.

This is not an ordinary angelic encounter—as if any angelic encounter can be called "ordinary." This is God Himself, as evidenced by the command to Joshua to remove his sandals, which he did, before bowing down in worship. Joshua would not have worshipped an angel. God had come to enlist Joshua in His heavenly army. He was telling him, as He had told Moses, *"Now therefore go, and I will be with your mouth, and teach you what you shall say"* (Exodus 4:12). The Commander proceeded to give Joshua the tactics for the taking of Jericho, the mighty and miraculous conquest that gave the people of Israel a firm foothold in the land of Canaan.

In one of our meetings, while people were receiving prayer at the altar, a man looked up to see something he had never seen before. It caught him by complete surprise. His spiritual eyes were opened to see a heavenly being, the size of a man, six feet tall, who seemed to be hovering over the altar area and ministering to the people who were receiving prayer. What he saw clearly was the movement of the air, even though the angelic figure wasn't completely defined. He was awestruck by this moment, and he defined it as the moment he became more aware of spiritual realities.

Some years ago, I remember ministering in a place that was swirling with angelic activity. After an intense overnight angelic encounter involving a great quantity of supernatural oil, I arrived at the early morning session ready to preach and minister. Before I could finish my message, supernatural oil began to drip from my hands. I asked the people to form a prayer circle around the outside edge of the room so that I could lay hands on each person. As I did so, miracles began to occur. Some people were healed physically, others emotionally or spiritually.

The worship leader, who had been maintaining a continual stream of worship music in the background, became so overwhelmed by the presence of God in the room that he took his hands off the keyboard and fell to the floor. The music did not stop! In a short time, we began to hear angelic voices singing along with a supernatural accompaniment. We later confirmed that this music had not been recorded or programmed ahead of time.

I look back on that day as the beginning of a new outpouring of the Holy Spirit when revival visited many people in many places. God's heavenly army was on the move!

ANGEL PRAYER

Heavenly Father, I acknowledge You as the Supreme Commander of angel armies, and I worship You for moving on behalf of people on earth who belong to You. I agree with Your purposes and I align myself with the angels You have assigned to my portion of the kingdom, praying that Your unseen forces will move to bring an increase of breakthrough and revival. Astonish us with the outpouring of Your glory! In Jesus's powerful name, amen.

13

CAN ANIMALS HELP US TO SEE ANGELS?

An angel confronted Balaam and his donkey.

But God was very angry when he went, and the angel of the LORD stood in the road to oppose him. Balaam was riding on his donkey, and his two servants were with him. When the donkey saw the angel of the LORD standing in the road with a drawn sword in his hand, it turned off the road into a field. Balaam beat it to get it back on the road. Then the angel of the LORD stood in a narrow path through the vineyards, with walls on both sides. When the donkey saw the angel of the LORD, it pressed close to the wall, crushing Balaam's foot against it. So he beat the donkey again. Then the angel of the LORD moved on ahead and stood in a narrow place where there was no room to turn, either to the right or to the left. When the donkey saw the angel of the LORD, it lay down under Balaam, and he was angry and beat it with his staff. Then the LORD opened the donkey's mouth, and it said to Balaam, "What have I done to

*you to make you beat me these three times?" Balaam answered
the donkey, "You have made a fool of me! If only I had a sword
in my hand, I would kill you right now." The donkey said to
Balaam, "Am I not your own donkey, which you have always
ridden, to this day? Have I been in the habit of doing this to
you?" "No," he said. Then the LORD opened Balaam's eyes,
and he saw the angel of the LORD standing in the road with his
sword drawn. So he bowed low and fell facedown. The angel of
the LORD asked him, "Why have you beaten your donkey these
three times? I have come here to oppose you because your path is
a reckless one before me. The donkey saw me and turned away
from me these three times. If it had not turned away, I would
certainly have killed you by now, but I would have spared it."
Balaam said to the angel of the LORD, "I have sinned. I did not
realize you were standing in the road to oppose me. Now if you
are displeased, I will go back." The angel of the LORD said to
Balaam, "Go with the men, but speak only what I tell you." So
Balaam went with Balak's officials.*

(Numbers 22:22–35 NIV)

Balaam was acting foolishly, so God sent an angel to turn him
back. The only problem was that Balaam could not see the angel,
although his donkey could. Eventually, God had to enable the
animal to speak in order to open Balaam's eyes to the reality before
him.

Is this merely an unusual story about an exceptional situation,
or does it have an application for you and me? We are responsible
only to see what God is revealing to us, but what can we do with
insufficient information?

Discerning the subtle changes in your atmosphere will help you connect with what is happening on a spiritual level, and it seems to me that animals are very good at this! If Balaam would've paid more attention to his donkey, it may have saved him from being rebuked by the angel. We know that dogs have a very sensitive sense of smell. New research suggests that dogs can actually detect many types of viruses, bacteria, and even signs of cancer in humans long before medical science is able to detect it.[1] I've also noticed that they are keenly aware of not just physical but also spiritual changes. Paying attention to their response could actually help you greatly.

In his book, *Angels on Assignment*, Pastor Rolland Buck related many stories about how his dog, Queenie, would often interact with the angels that had come to visit him. Recounting one instance he said, "As Gabriel was talking with me, Chroni, the other angel, played with Queenie, tickling her ears, getting her on her back and having fun with her. Queenie lapped it up! I wish she could talk because I would like to know what her impressions were."[2]

We used to have a friendly neighbor named Phyllis who lived beside us. She loved bringing her little dog named Fluffy over to our home to visit us, because she noticed that Fluffy could discern the Lord and loved His presence that surrounded our lives. Fluffy's reaction to the spiritual dimension helped Phyllis to see that the supernatural realm was real.

1. Joana Cavaco Silva, "Can dogs detect cancer?" (reviewed by Vincent J. Tavella, MPH), November 7, 2018, Medical News Today, https://www.medicalnewstoday.com/articles/323620.php#overview (accessed January 24, 2020).
2. Roland Buck, *Angels on Assignment* (New Kensington, PA: Whitaker House, 2005), 44.

I commonly see angels in silhouette form, and I cannot always discern their defining details. I have learned to respond based on what I *can* discern, acting based on that partial information. When I do so, more comes. It takes a certain amount of faith to do that, but such faith is rewarded. Each of us can do the same.

ANGEL PRAYER

Heavenly Father, don't let me hold back from saying or doing Your will simply because I do not yet quite grasp the whole message. In reality, I never will be able to grasp it. Grant me an increase of faith and the anointing I need to risk speaking out when I cannot see the complete picture. Give me eyes to see Your angels when they come. In Jesus's holy name, amen.

14

DO WHATEVER IT TAKES TO COOPERATE

An angel confronted the people of Israel.

The angel of the LORD went up from Gilgal to Bokim and said, "I brought you up out of Egypt and led you into the land

I swore to give to your ancestors. I said, 'I will never break my covenant with you, and you shall not make a covenant with the people of this land, but you shall break down their altars.' Yet you have disobeyed me. Why have you done this? And I have also said, 'I will not drive them out before you; they will become traps for you, and their gods will become snares to you.'" When the angel of the LORD had spoken these things to all the Israelites, the people wept aloud, and they called that place Bokim. There they offered sacrifices to the LORD.

(Judges 2:1–5 NIV)

The angel of the Lord scolded the people of Israel as a group, and it appears that every one of them heard the stern message. This is worth noting.

Although angels seem to be able to speak whatever language is required for communication and their appearances often are accompanied by manifestations that will draw people's attention, not necessarily everyone in a group can see or hear them. Think of the number of scriptural accounts of angel encounters, or encounters with the Spirit in which only one or a select few individuals understood what was happening. (See Daniel 10:7; John 12:29; Acts 9:7.)

When angels come into the midst of a group of people and only some can see or hear them, the others can find their way toward a clearer awareness and comprehension if they turn to the Lord and ask for help.

In Australia, I was teaching about angels in an auditorium. From the platform, I noticed an angel in the back of the room, leaning against the wall. He was so tall, his head nearly touched the ceiling. I said, "In the back, right there, I see a tall angel." People turned around to look. Some people could see it, but others could not. One man told me later that he was unable to see the angel, but he thought of an ingenious way to capture the moment. With his smart phone, he took a selfie in front of the place I had pointed to. When he looked at the photo, what he had been unable to see with his natural eyes, he could now see clearly—there was the big angel behind him in the picture, filled with vibrant light.

When angels come with a message from heaven, it's up to us to hear, receive, and believe what they're saying. Do whatever it takes to cooperate with a combination of God-given discernment and creative inspiration!

ANGEL PRAYER

Heavenly Father, I make it my prayer right now—before my next opportunity to encounter an angel in a group setting—that You will grant me the ability to be one of the ones who can see and hear the heavenly messenger. Make it real for me, I pray. Equip me with eyes to see and ears to hear, and the faith to believe. Thanking You in advance, I pray in the name of Your Son, Jesus, amen.

15

OPEN THE EYES OF YOUR HEART

An angel called Gideon to lead the battle against his enemies.

The angel of the LORD came and sat down under the oak in Ophrah that belonged to Joash the Abiezrite, where his son Gideon was threshing wheat in a winepress to keep it from the Midianites. When the angel of the LORD appeared to Gideon, he said, "The LORD is with you, mighty warrior." "Pardon me, my lord," Gideon replied, "but if the LORD is with us, why has all this happened to us? Where are all his wonders that our ancestors told us about when they said, 'Did not the LORD bring us up out of Egypt?' But now the LORD has abandoned us and given us into the hand of Midian." The LORD turned to him and said, "Go in the strength you have and save Israel out of Midian's hand. Am I not sending you?" "Pardon me, my lord," Gideon replied, "but how can I save Israel? My clan is the weakest in Manasseh, and I am the least in my family." The LORD answered, "I will be with you, and you will strike down all the Midianites, leaving none alive." Gideon replied, "If now I have found favor in your eyes, give me a sign that it is really you talking to me. Please do not go away until I come back and bring my offering and set it before you." And the LORD said, "I will wait until you return." Gideon went inside, prepared a young goat, and from an ephah of flour he made bread without yeast. Putting the meat in a basket and its broth in a pot, he brought them out and offered them to

him under the oak. The angel of God said to him, "Take the
meat and the unleavened bread, place them on this rock, and
pour out the broth." And Gideon did so. Then the angel of the
Lord touched the meat and the unleavened bread with the
tip of the staff that was in his hand. Fire flared from the rock,
consuming the meat and the bread. And the angel of the Lord
disappeared. When Gideon realized that it was the angel of
the Lord, he exclaimed, "Alas, Sovereign Lord! I have seen
the angel of the Lord face to face!"　(Judges 6:11–22 niv)

It took a while for Gideon to realize that the "person" who had
come to him was, in fact, the angel of the Lord. Gideon was just an
ordinary, hardworking fellow, and, like many of us, he lacked practice in using his spiritual senses. How can we sharpen our spiritual
senses so that we don't miss angelic visitations?

Spiritual sight is both a gift to be received and a discipline to
be developed. We can actually practice and grow in our ability to
discern angels. Our best starting place is worship. As we worship
God, we move out of our visible, earthly realm. As we pray, "Open
the eyes of my heart, Lord," He will answer.

A pastor told me about a time when she woke up in the wee hours
of the morning during a storm. She could hear music playing somewhere in her house, and yet she could not find the source. It sounded
like a violin and a trumpet playing along with some other instruments.
As the quiet music continued to play all day long, she began to think
she was just hearing things. But when her friend came over and asked,
"Where is that music coming from?" she knew it must be angels
bringing them peace in the midst of a long and dangerous storm. In
fact, the music ceased about the same time the weather cleared.

All of us can be aware of God and His holy angels—anywhere, anytime. We just need to know what to look for and pay attention—and practice tuning in.

ANGEL PRAYER

Dear heavenly Father, You are Lord of the angels and the Lord of my life. I must have more of Your presence! I pray that You will open the eyes of my heart to sense Your nearness so that I can catch glimpses—and more—of Your heavenly messengers. I need Your Holy Spirit to remind me to pay attention. Praying in Jesus's name, amen.

16

GUIDELINES FROM HEAVEN

An angel appeared to Manoah's wife to announce Samson's birth and to give special instructions.

The angel of the LORD appeared to her and said, "You are barren and childless, but you are going to become pregnant and give birth to a son. Now see to it that you drink no wine or other fermented drink and that you do not eat anything

unclean. You will become pregnant and have a son whose
head is never to be touched by a razor because the boy is to be
a Nazirite, dedicated to God from the womb. He will take the
lead in delivering Israel from the hands of the Philistines."

(Judges 13:3–5 NIV)

All of Scripture is meant to show us something about the ways of God. This passage shows us that angels intervene in people's daily lives so that believers will be able to fulfill their eternal destiny. *"Are* [angels] *not all ministering spirits, sent forth to minister for them who shall be heirs of salvation?"* (Hebrews 1:14). Apart from the intervention of the angel of the Lord, Manoah's wife would not have had a clue about what was happening or how to raise this special son.

In the days ahead, I believe that the only way we will be able to survive will be by means of the supernatural mediation of the Holy Spirit, which will often include the ministry of angels. This is so important that my wife Janet and I have established the International Glory Institute to train students using both in-person and online teachings. We want everyone to know how to operate in the supernatural realm and how to engage with God Himself as well as with the angels who are at our service. That is also the reason for the books and other resources I have made available, including this very book.

Several times in my life, I have met an angel who initially appeared to be just a stranger. Angels have come to help me in an airport, to escort me through rush-hour traffic, and as an informative "person" on the side of the road. I'm not talking about just regular people, about whom you might say, "Oh, that one is such an angel." I am talking about actual angels, disguised as regular people.

I'm sure we have all met angels like this! We just didn't recognize them as angels.

ANGEL PRAYER

Come once more, Father, as You have done in the past for people of all descriptions. Make me a good receiver of Your heavenly messages and help me walk in joyful obedience in response to whatever You say. If I need to relinquish a deficient worldview or something specific that gets in the way of my ability to receive, please show me what to do about it. I trust You! Through Your Son Jesus. Amen.

17

DO YOU KNOW YOUR ANGEL'S NAME?

The angel appeared to Manoah and his wife to give them instructions about Samson's birth and upbringing.

God hearkened to the voice of Manoah; and the angel of God came again unto the woman as she sat in the field: but Manoah her husband was not with her. And the woman *made haste, and ran, and told her husband, and said unto him, Behold, the man hath appeared unto me, that came unto me the other day. And Manoah arose, and went after his wife, and came to the man, and said unto him, Art thou the man that spakest unto the woman? And he said, I am. And Manoah said, Now let thy words come to pass: what shall be the ordering of the child, and how shall we do unto him? And the angel of Jehovah said unto Manoah, Of all that I said unto the woman let her beware. She may not eat of anything that cometh of the vine, neither let her drink wine or strong drink, nor eat any unclean thing; all that I commanded her let her observe. And Manoah said unto the angel of Jehovah, I pray thee, let us detain thee, that we may make ready a kid for thee. And the angel of Jehovah said unto Manoah, Though thou detain me, I will not eat of thy bread; and if thou wilt make ready a burnt-offering, thou must offer it unto Jehovah. For Manoah knew not that he was the angel of Jehovah. And Manoah said unto the angel of Jehovah, What is thy name, that, when thy words come to pass, we may do thee honor? And the angel of Jehovah said unto him, **Wherefore askest thou after my name, seeing it is wonderful?** So Manoah took the kid with the meal-offering, and offered it upon the rock unto Jehovah: and the angel did wondrously, and Manoah and his wife looked on. For it came to pass, when the flame went up toward heaven from off the altar, that the angel of Jehovah ascended in the flame of the altar: and Manoah and his wife looked on; and they fell on their faces to the ground. But the angel of Jehovah did no*

more appear to Manoah or to his wife. Then Manoah knew
that he was the angel of Jehovah. (Judges 13:9–21 ASV)

God's message became even more specific. His angel visited Manoah's wife a second time, and this time, she fetched her husband, who engaged the angel of the Lord in an instructive conversation. They did not realize they had been speaking with the very angel of God until the end of their interaction––and by then, all they could do was fall on their faces in awe. Having secured their cooperation, the angel's words came true and the couple did have a son named Samson.

Here, the angel of the Lord told Manoah that His name was "Wonderful," and we must understand, angels often reveal their names if we ask. (See Luke 1:19.). Angels can have descriptive names that relate to their assignments, such as Harvest, Healing, Deliverance, or Abundance. Or they can have ordinary sounding names, such as Dana or Ryan—names that carry specific meanings.

After reading my book *Seeing Angels*, my friend Pastor Desiree felt challenged to ask her angels for their names. Before she read my book, she never realized that this was something that was possible to do! But it is! So she did it! The answer she received thrilled her heart to no end. Her first angel said his name was "Miracles," and her second angel said that his name was "More Miracles"! She told me, "When Miracles comes, More Miracles follows!" And this is exactly the way it works in her life. God has given her a tremendous miracle ministry. Every opportunity we've had to sit under her teaching, we've seen Pastor Desiree and her angels in action as the miracles flow easily from heaven.

My personal angels have revealed their names to me, and I can see how they are connected with the purpose of my life. If you wish, ask the angels who have been assigned to you to share their names. They may whisper it gently into your ear, or you may begin to see a specific word repetitively or feel the strong impression of a name in your spirit. Don't rush it; such insights will usually come when you are relaxed, such as when you are just waking up from sleep or just going about your day without trying too hard to make a spiritual connection. It is totally possible for you to learn your angel's name, and I believe you will as you open up and begin to listen!

ANGEL PRAYER

Heavenly Father, thank You for Your abundant provision for me. Thank You for assigning angels to my life who have specific roles to play, and for giving them names to match. Help me catch sight of my personal angels and open my comprehension to grasp their names. I want to cooperate with my heavenly messengers to the fullest extent possible, as You enable me. In Jesus's name, amen.

18

COMMANDING ANGELS THROUGH CHRIST'S AUTHORITY

An angel was sent to afflict the people of David's time.

So the LORD sent a plague on Israel from that morning until the end of the time designated, and seventy thousand of the people from Dan to Beersheba died. When the angel stretched out his hand to destroy Jerusalem, the LORD relented concerning the disaster and said to the angel who was afflicting the people, "Enough! Withdraw your hand." The angel of the LORD was then at the threshing floor of Araunah the Jebusite. When David saw the angel who was striking down the people, he said to the LORD, "I have sinned; I, the shepherd, have done wrong. These are but sheep. What have they done? Let your hand fall on me and my family."

(2 Samuel 24:15–17 NIV)

Through the Scriptures, we can see that David was very familiar with angelic activity.

David writes in Psalms, *"For he will command his angels concerning you to guard you in all your ways"* (Psalm 91:11 NIV).

Here, we see that God does the commanding. However, as believers in whom God's Spirit dwells, we must also recognize that we do possess spiritual rights and authority.

On earth, Jesus was, for a while, *"made a little lower than the angels"* (Hebrews 2:9), but after He sacrificed Himself on the cross, He was crowned with glory and honor. It is plain to see that angels are subject to Him. Yet where does He live? In the hearts of believers. *"God has chosen to make known among the Gentiles the glorious riches of this mystery, which is Christ in you, the hope of glory"* (Colossians 1:27 NIV).

With Christ Jesus living inside us, we are privileged to share His glory! Thus, we have the right to speak by His authority. God's old covenant people didn't have any authority to command angels. Today, under the New Covenant, we do, as He leads. (See 1 Peter 3:22; Matthew 16:19; 18:18.) The Scriptures even say that we will judge angels. (See 1 Corinthians 6:3.) You cannot be a judge unless you have legal authority. When we decree the Word of God, angels move.

Contrary to what some people have taught, I have never felt comfortable with the idea of directly commanding angels by speaking their names or calling on them directly. This seems too dangerous to me, because angels never desire to bring glory to themselves. They are present in our lives to bring glory and honor to God. We should learn how to command our angels by calling upon the powerful name of Jesus. We can successfully command angels by prayer directed to God and by speaking through Christ's authority. Here is an example:

My wife Janet and I received a desperate phone call from a dear friend who lives in the Canadian Arctic. Her husband and son had gone hunting on snowmobiles, but had been overtaken by a blizzard. The situation looked grave. Our friend asked us to pray. We know that angels love the Word of God and, when they hear us speaking God's words, they agree with them and move according to their decrees.

As Janet and I spoke God's promises over the missing men, we could sense angels going forth. We asked others to pray with us. Before long, the men were rescued and they had an amazing story to tell:

As they had huddled together under a tarp between their two snowmobiles, approaching the last stages of hypothermia, they heard a man and a woman talking. The woman seemed to be Swedish and the man appeared to be Hispanic. They had appeared out of nowhere, apparently on foot, in the midst of the blizzard. "Wake up! Wake up! You can't go to sleep!" shouted the man. Roused from near death, the two hunters began to converse with the unusual couple. The conversation didn't make much sense and the men could not figure out how this couple had gotten there, but it served its purpose—to keep them awake and alive until a search team could rescue them. As the team arrived on the scene, the foreigners wandered off into the snow. Were they angels? No one can explain it any other way. (Later, I found out that one of the men gave the two angels fun nicknames based on what nationality they seemed to be: "José" for the Hispanic man and "Ingrid" for the Swedish woman!)

ANGEL PRAYER

Heavenly Father, it excites me to think of what might happen the next time angelic intervention is required!

You are amazing. Keep me attentive to Your Spirit all the time so I will remember your Word and know how to pray. In the name of Jesus, amen.

19

AN ENORMOUS ANGEL WITH A SWORD OF CORRECTION

The angel of the Lord confronted David about his sin of numbering the people.

> *And David lifted up his eyes, and saw the angel of the LORD stand between the earth and the heaven, having a drawn sword in His hand stretched out over Jerusalem. Then David and the elders of Israel, who were clothed in sackcloth, fell upon their faces.*　　　　(1 Chronicles 21:16)

Because He loves us so much, God cares about our sin, which separates us from Him. And since we often fail to notice when we have crossed the line into sin, and thus will rarely think to ask God to correct us, He, at times, sends us His message in a way guaranteed to get our attention—through an angel.

The angel of the Lord can be especially fearsome to behold. In this case, David, who listened to Satan and numbered the people of Israel, had regretted his sin as God's angel began meting out justice, slaughtering people across the land. Jerusalem was next. David was beside himself. "Take me instead! The people didn't sin! I did!" That's when he saw the enormous angel with his sword stretched out over the city. At that point, God commanded the angel to stay his hand and, in turn, God helped David to regain his righteous footing before Him.

In His mercy, God holds back full punishment when we turn from our sin, and I believe He sends angelic assistance more often than we realize. A woman I know once felt God was telling her (somewhat like the prophet Nathan) to confront a close friend about an ongoing sin. It was delicate business because this friend was her respected mentor, old enough to be her mother. But she felt she was the only one who could speak to the issue. With resolve and prayerful trepidation, she set up a time to meet with her friend.

While she was sleeping the night before, a slight noise awakened her. She opened her eyes and saw the heads of two angels, next to her bed in dim silhouette. She heard one say to the other, "Is she going to do it?" The other replied, "Yes."

Somehow, she knew that her friend's angel was meeting with hers—and allowing their little conversation to be overheard so that she would feel their support. The next day, she found just the right tactful words to bring up the sensitive matter, and her friend's heart was receptive. Righteousness prevailed all around. Surely, the angels were also there, nodding their approval.

ANGEL PRAYER

Heavenly Father, I bow humbly at Your feet, and I pray that You will keep my spirit attentive enough to Your still, small voice so that I will never need sharp correction from You. But if I do, please send an angel of mercy to assist me to see the truth and keep me from suffering destructive consequences. I need Your help every hour of every day, through Jesus's all-powerful name, amen.

20

ANGEL FOOD CAKE IS A REAL THING!

An angel was sent to comfort and encourage Elijah and prepare him for the future.

> *As he lay and slept under a juniper tree, behold, then an angel touched him, and said to him, Arise and eat. And he looked, and, behold, there was a cake baked on the coals, and a cruse of water at his head. And he did eat and drink, and laid him down again. And the angel of the LORD came again*

the second time, and touched him, and said, Arise and eat;
because the journey is too great for you. (1 Kings 19:5–7)

Elijah was exhausted. He had just vanquished the prophets of Baal on Mount Carmel (see 1 Kings 18:16–46), and then he had run a marathon. He was too far gone to ask God for help. Even his mighty faith was panting for breath.

So, twice, an angel—unrequested and unexpected—brought Elijah room service under a juniper tree. He needed every drop of that water and every crumb of that cake. That supernaturally provided food flooded him with the strength he needed to go to Mount Horeb, a tough forty days' journey on foot. God had a lot more for Elijah to do, and He knew he couldn't do it without angelic support.

Angels can and will bring us what we need, "out of nowhere." After hearing what angels did for Elijah at various points in his life, you have to believe modern accounts. When the angels put away our Christmas decorations and cleaned our house (see the second entry in this book, "Angels Bring Divine Provision"), one reason I was sure it was angels was that everything was put away perfectly. Nobody on the face of the earth knew how and where I kept everything. Leave it to angels to do a perfect job!

An elderly lady told me what had happened to her. She said, "I think God has painting angels. I needed my house painted, but I didn't have the money, strength, or ability to do it. I prayed, and when I woke up in the morning, the house was painted. I can't explain it. God's painting angels must have done it."

When I shared these stories, a special friend and mentor of mine remarked that her house had a plumbing problem. The roots of trees had grown into her sewer pipes, clogging them. It would have been too expensive to hire someone to take care of it. She said, "I guess we need plumbing angels to make a house call."

I said, "Well, let's release them." Without anyone ever seeing their activity, angels must have come. The tree roots were cleared out and the problem was completely resolved.

I'm sure these stories sound unbelievable to some people. If you doubt them, just think of Elijah and his "angel food" cakes. *"Taste and see that the LORD is good,"* (Psalm 34:8). Take it to Him in prayer and listen to what He tells you.

ANGEL PRAYER

Heavenly Father, show me what kinds of provision You want to send to me by means of angels. Put Your ideas into my mind so that I can pray and release the angels who are standing ready. I don't want to put limits on You. You created the universe, after all, and You have not changed. You are still limitless and loving and powerful. Expand my horizons and increase my faith. In Jesus's name, amen.

21

LISTEN TO THE SPECIFIC INSTRUCTIONS

An angel told Elijah what to say to an evil king.

The angel of the LORD said to Elijah the Tishbite, "Go up and meet the messengers of the king of Samaria and ask them, 'Is it because there is no God in Israel that you are going off to consult Baal-Zebub, the god of Ekron?'"   (2 Kings 1:3 NIV)

The son of the evil King Ahab was named Ahaziah, and he became king of Samaria upon his father's death. When he injured himself badly by falling from his upstairs room, it never occurred to him to seek God. Instead, he sent messengers to the god of Ekron, Baal-Zebub, to inquire as to whether or not he would recover. They set out on their errand. That's when the angel intervened, speaking to Elijah the words above.

Elijah met Ahaziah's messengers on the road and used those exact words to greet them. They did not know this was the great prophet, their master's nemesis. How could this strange man have known what they had been told to do? Then Elijah finished his message to the messengers by saying that their master would surely die of his injuries.

So they turned around and went back to Ahaziah, who was surprised to see them back so soon. He was furious to discover that Elijah had intercepted his messengers to deliver a message from the God of Israel. God's messenger (the angel) had done his job well.

Just as Elijah had to cooperate with the instructions given to him by God's angel, so do we need to cooperate when we receive instruction. Angels never teach; their instruction is not of that nature. God expects you and me to learn from the Holy Spirit Himself, who comes to anoint us, fill us, and lead us into all truth. God's Word can teach us everything we need to know.

Angelic instruction is usually more along the lines of "go here and do this." They go where God sends them to undertake specific actions. They deliver divine strategies, instructions, insights, and wisdom, not long theological speeches.

The angel Gabriel instructed the virgin girl, Mary, telling her in detail that she would become pregnant by the power of the Holy Spirit and bear the Messiah. He told her what to name her Son, what He would do, and that her barren cousin Elizabeth was also miraculously pregnant. (See Luke 1:26–37.) He didn't teach her about Israel's messianic hope or how to believe in God. That information had to come from somewhere else.

When Peter was in prison, a "jailbreak angel" struck his side in order to wake him up and break him out. His words were to the point: *"Quick, get up!"* (Acts 12:7 NIV). Then, as the chains dropped off Peter's wrists, the angel's instructions continued, *"Put on your clothes and sandals,"* which he did, and *"wrap your cloak around you and follow me"* (verse 8 NIV).

ANGEL PRAYER

Heavenly Father, I say "Bring it on, Lord!" I am wide open to hearing words of angelic instruction. I know already that angels often communicate wordlessly, if they communicate at all, but since they are Your messengers, I also expect to hear directive instructions. Would You please give an angel a message for me sometime soon? Help me tune my heart to Yours and remain alert for angelic messengers. Thank You ahead of time. In Jesus's name, amen.

22

ON GOD'S ORDERS

An angel instructed Elijah to go with a military representative of the king of Samaria.

The angel of the LORD said to Elijah, Go down with him: be not afraid of him. And he arose, and went down with him to the king.   (2 Kings 1:15)

Elijah had reason to be afraid of the king, since this was evil King Ahaziah, son of the ruthless King Ahab, who was out for the prophet's blood. Up to this point in the story, Elijah had remained at a safe distance, and when the king's messengers (in battalions of fifty military men) twice came to summon him, he had called down fire from heaven, killing them all.

Then, abruptly, the angel gave Elijah new instructions. Ahaziah had sent a fresh posse under a captain who, quaking with fear, dropped to his knees to summon Elijah. The angel said, "This time, go to the king. You do not need to be afraid of him." Elijah gathered up the skirts of his robe and went as summoned, carrying the same prophetic message as before: "Dire news, O king: You are going to die of your recent injuries." And then he must have walked free, leaving behind a dying king who would no longer be a threat to him.

Why did the Lord seem to change His mind? Was it something about the timing? I do not have a good answer to that question. But the point about obedience to God's instructions is clear: we must obey only what God's heavenly messengers say, and obey human messengers only when their words match God's.

Even when the Lord sends us encouragement by angelic means, He does so when and how He chooses. Recently, I joined a group of ministers for a special conference in Quaqtaq, Nunavik, a village in northern Quebec. One night, an anointed evangelist named Hattie ministered to us, and I couldn't help but notice a tall angel with large wings standing behind her, filled with white light. When I turned to my wife to ask her if she could see it, the angel disappeared, only to reappear about fifteen minutes later. I mentioned it to Hattie after the service, and she was greatly encouraged. She said that an angel named John had been assigned to her during her pastoral ordination in 1995, and that she often felt John strengthening her, but for a long time, she had not felt him. Earlier that same day, she had asked the Lord if John was still with her. Now, even though she herself had not felt him, she was reassured that he was still working in her life.

Do you realize that once God has assigned an angel to your life, he will never take that angel or his assignment away from you? Remember what Romans 11:29 says: *"For God's gifts and his call can never be withdrawn"* (NLT).

ANGEL PRAYER

Heavenly Father and Lord, You are the King of kings and I bow to You. Your word is my command. Keep me sensitive to shifts in Your instructions, even when they seem to contradict previous instructions. Send Your angels to tip me off before I make mistakes. Keep me in the center of Your will at all times. I depend on You for everything. Amen.

23

DO YOU HAVE EYES TO SEE?

Angels protected Elisha and his servant.

> *And when the servant of the man of God was risen early, and gone forth, behold, a host compassed the city both with horses and chariots. And his servant said to him, Alas, my master! how shall we do? And he answered, Fear not: for they that be with us are more than they that be with them. And Elisha prayed, and said, Lord, I pray You, open his eyes, that he may see." And the Lord opened the eyes of the young man; and he saw: and, behold, the mountain was full of horses and chariots of fire round about Elisha.* (2 Kings 6:15–17)

The angel army was spread across the mountainside as far as the eye could see—*if* a person had eyes to see them. Elisha's servant couldn't see the chariots of fire until God opened the eyes of his spirit. They were real, but invisible otherwise.

With the gift of discerning of spirits (see 1 Corinthians 12:10), you have the power to see into the spiritual realm. It's similar to having the ability to understand Jesus's parables. When His disciples asked Him why He used stories to explain things, Jesus replied, *"Because the knowledge of the secrets of the kingdom of heaven has been given to you, but not to them"* (Matthew 13:11 NIV).

The privilege of knowing God's inside information is a gift that has been granted to those who believe—even though many of us are like Elisha's servant, just the same. We need divine eye surgery in order to access the gift and see into the spiritual realm. God's light must shine upon our human minds to help us see spiritual realities. Such comprehension cannot be mastered by human education or effort. The gift of discerning of spirits, like all spiritual gifts, is just that—a gift of the Spirit.

One way to further our ability to see into the spiritual realm is to be willing to testify to what God has done. When he visited heaven, the angel told John, *"The testimony of Jesus is the spirit of prophecy"* (Revelation 19:10). In other words, when we speak about what God has done, we create an opening in the Spirit world for Him to do more. The more we speak about angel marvels, the more we will see them!

Once, when I was new to all of this, I was speaking about the glory of God in front of a group. We were meeting in a place that had an old-fashioned stage and I was standing on the floor in front of it. People in the audience began to buzz and point at something behind me. I turned and saw an amazing sight: the heavy stage curtains were wildly swaying back and forth, and it looked like a giant was doing it. Some people, assuming it was just a stagehand playing around, went behind the curtain to investigate. There was no one there. In any case, the movement was much too forceful to have been caused by a human or natural cause.

For those of us who were just beginning to understand about God's glory, this was just the kind of an angelic encounter to have. Now we could testify about that as well!

Recently, while I was on a book tour speaking about *Seeing Angels*, night after night, people began reporting having special encounters with angels. While waiting in the book signing line in

Albuquerque, New Mexico, a small white feather fell on the back of a blue shirt worn by a man named Hank, while others in the line watched in awe. Two days later, while I was in Sanford, Florida, another small feather appeared on the corner of the *Seeing Angels* book as a woman named Cindy was waiting in line to speak with me. These feathers are heavenly signs—indicators that angels are not only near but working to accelerate God's promises in your life. Both Hank and Cindy were individually encouraged by this sign and left our encounter with a higher expectancy for the supernatural! Speak in the Spirit, and then see in the Spirit!

ANGEL PRAYER

Heavenly Father, as Your faithful child and servant, I pray in Your name. I ask You to open my eyes to see the spiritual reality that is all around me. Where I remain a little uncertain, introduce me to the activity and presence of angels, little by little. One thing I know for sure: Your glory realm is ever-present, whether I can see it or not. Keep me looking in Your direction without fail. Praying in the name of Jesus, amen.

24

RELEASE THE ANGEL WARRIORS

An angel saved the Israelites from the Assyrians.

And it came to pass that night, that the angel of the LORD went out, and smote in the camp of the Assyrians a hundred fourscore and five thousand: and when they arose early in the morning, behold, they were all dead corpses. (2 Kings 19:35)

God's people in Judah faced annihilation at the hands of the fearsome Assyrian army. The Assyrian king, Sennacherib, was laying siege to Jerusalem, after having conquered all of the Israelite cities in the north. He openly ridiculed Judah for opposing him and for trusting in their God. Good King Hezekiah prayed humbly and fervently, and God heard his prayer. Through the prophet Isaiah, God promised that the Israelites would prevail against impossible odds.

Arrogant as always, Sennacherib disregarded God's word and drew his vast army into position. But during the night, the angel of the Lord swept through the troops, slaughtering 185,000 men. At dawn, the defenders of Jerusalem saw a sea of corpses, and Sennacherib was fleeing with the remnants of his army.

You and I will never find ourselves in the same position as Hezekiah and his city of Jerusalem, but we certainly face spiritual combat. We need to know that angels intervene on our behalf, for the most part, in unseen ways. In the battle between right and wrong, they hold up God's standard of truth, against which no enemy can triumph.

We see this kind of combat throughout Scripture. God did not spare the Egyptians at the time of the Exodus, saying to the Israelites, *"Behold, I send an angel before you, to keep you in the way, and to bring you into the place which I have prepared"* (Exodus 23:20). These angels of battle carry powerful swords that make *Star Wars* light sabers look like nothing. Even brave King David was afraid of them: *"But David...was afraid because of the sword of the angel of the LORD"* (1 Chronicles 21:30).

The apostle John witnessed angelic combat in the heavenly realm: *"Then war broke out in heaven. Michael and his angels fought against the dragon, and the dragon and his angels fought back"* (Revelation 12:7 NIV).

Beware, enemies of God! *"Let them be as chaff before the wind: and let the angel of the LORD chase them. Let their way be dark and slippery: and let the angel of the LORD persecute them. For without cause have they hidden for me their net in a pit, which without cause they have dug for my soul"* (Psalm 35:5–7).

The battle belongs to the Lord and His angels: *"The angel of the LORD encamps round about them that fear Him, and delivers them"* (Psalm 34:7).

While I was ministering in Albuquerque, New Mexico, a young Navajo girl named Mikalynne drew the most beautiful picture of me. In the Spirit, her eyes were opened to see a warrior angel standing right behind me as I ministered. In his hand, he held a large, imposing sword that was surely ready to battle any evil assignment intended against me. This has happened on several occasions, when other people have seen these warrior angels around me and let me know about it. Maybe some people have told you that they see angels around you as well?

If you're a child of God, He's got angels watching over you for sure. I was so delighted to receive this picture from Mikalynne after the meeting because it brought me great encouragement to see this large angel standing behind me as I ministered God's Word. It gave me peace knowing that no matter what plans the enemy has made, God's plans are always better and His angels are always surrounding my life, working in our ministry, girded and fully equipped to face any battle that might arise. They hold the weapons for war in their hands so that my hands can be lifted freely to worship the Lord and give Him glory.

Often in our Angel Schools, I encourage people to draw the angels that they see in the Spirit. Not everybody is an artist, and for some, this takes a real step of faith to put their pencil to the paper. But I've noticed that when a person begins drawing what they've seen in the Spirit, something very special that happens. Their physical eyes begin to see what their spiritual eyes have beheld. It helps to bring visionary alignment to the spirit, soul and body.

I would encourage you to try this the next time you receive a clear vision in the spirit realm. Draw it as you see it, write it down so you can see and grasp the reality of what God has made known to you.

ANGEL PRAYER

You, heavenly Father, command angel armies. When evil tries to stand before You, Your angels cut it down. I don't particularly enjoy spiritual combat, yet I am grateful that Your angels defend me at every turn without my knowing it. Preserve my earthly life and the lives of my brothers and sisters by keeping us on Your path of truth. Alert us to the enemy's deception and preserve us from drifting. I am Yours and I pray in Jesus's name. Amen.

25

FIERY ANGELS OF LIGHT

An angel brought atonement for Isaiah's sin.

> *Then one of the seraphim flew to me with a live coal in his hand, which he had taken with tongs from the altar. With it he touched my mouth and said, "See, this has touched your lips; your guilt is taken away and your sin atoned for."*
>
> (Isaiah 6:6–7 NIV)

A *seraph* is an order of angels called *seraphim*, which means "burning," "shining," or "fiery ones." Scripture clearly describes the seraphim as having six wings and emanating gloriously brilliant light. (See Isaiah 6:1–7.) Seraphim are only explicitly mentioned by name once in the Scriptures, but we can see them throughout the Bible whenever the fire of God is mentioned. (See 2 Kings 2:11, 6:17; Hebrews 1:7.) The seraphim serve as God's throne attendants, worshipping continually, saying, "Holy, holy, holy!"

God dispatched a seraph to touch Isaiah's lips with a burning coal, which cleansed the prophet from sin so he could do what God wanted him to do. It was a unique experience to be sure, but one that is not out of the realm of possibility for you and me. God's angels live in His holiness, and when they come into our lives, they desire for us to live in His holiness too. Nothing grieves an angel more than seeing a child of God trespassing down the dark pathway of sin. They can't *make* you live a holy life because God has given you a free will, which allows you to make your own decisions. But knowing that God's angels are always watching over us should make us want to live for the Lord, even when nobody else is watching. Seraphim surround us with an atmosphere of God's holiness that convicts us of our lack of faith and draws us closer to the loving presence of Jesus. These are the angels who are released to work with evangelism teams and can often be experienced at soul-winning meetings in which the focus is on salvation and living a consecrated life for Christ. Some people have reported feeling their presence as that of an instant sensation of heat on their heads, hands, or shoulders. Sometimes people's entire bodies change temperature when Seraphim draw near.

When my friend Mary K. Baxter sees angels as spirits rather than in human form, she says that they always look like fire to her. Many people share this common experience. Of all the different ways that these angels can appear and take form, I've found that they often manifest in the appearance of bright light. I've seen Seraphim on several occasions, and to me, they look like long, vertically-stretched flashes of light that emanate brilliance from their being, almost like an elongated, radiating star. The psalmist said, *"He makes...flames of fire his servants"* (Psalm 104:4 NIV). Seraphim serve the purposes of God. I believe they were present and active on the day of Pentecost, preparing the atmosphere for the arrival of the Holy Spirit. (See Acts 2:3.) When Seraphim appear, get ready for an encounter with the holiness and splendor of God. Seraphim are always involved when God's fire is required.

ANGEL PRAYER

Heavenly Father and God, I know that You dwell in unapproachable light that blinds our eyes from seeing You. (See 1 Timothy 6:16.) Yet I would welcome an encounter with Your fiery angels of light, both as a personal purification and as a spur to propel me to accomplish an assignment from You. I know You would sustain me through such an experience and that I would come out of it stronger, glorifying Your name ever more. According to Your will, position me to experience Your holy flames of fire through the seraphim. In Jesus's name, amen.

26

MILLIONS OF ANGELS STANDING BY

An angel saved Shadrach, Meshach, and Abednego from the fiery furnace.

Then Nebuchadnezzar the king was astonished, and rose up in haste, and spoke, and said to his counselors, Did not we cast three men bound into the midst of the fire? They answered and said to the king, True, O king. He answered and said, Lo, I see four men loose, walking in the midst of the fire, and they have no hurt; and the form of the fourth is like the Son of God. Then Nebuchadnezzar came near to the mouth of the burning fiery furnace, and spoke, and said, Shadrach, Meshach, and Abednego, you servants of the Most High God, come forth, and come here. Then Shadrach, Meshach, and Abednego, came forth of the midst of the fire. And the princes, governors, and captains, and the king's counselors, being gathered together, saw these men, upon whose bodies the fire had no power, nor was a hair of their head singed, neither were their coats changed, nor the smell of fire had passed on them. Then Nebuchadnezzar spoke, and said, Blessed be the God of Shadrach, Meshach, and Abednego, who has sent His angel, and delivered His servants that trusted in Him,

*and have changed the king's word, and yielded their bodies,
that they might not serve nor worship any god, except their
own God.*   (Daniel 3:24–28)

The glorious fourth man they had seen silhouetted against
the flames did not emerge from the mouth of the furnace with
Shadrach, Meshach, and Abednego because he was in fact an
angel. God had honored the faithfulness of Daniel's three friends
by rescuing them dramatically.

In one of Daniel's visions, he saw into heaven, where countless angels stood ready to be commanded. (See Daniel 7:10.) Had
this angel been dispatched because of the steady prayerfulness of
Daniel and his friends in the face of deadly threats? Can we expect
the same level of protection ourselves?

A young man in the Arctic named Nick once told me about
an encounter he had with an angel when he was just thirteen years
old. He had taken an ATV out to hunt caribou and had an accident on a muddy embankment. The vehicle flipped over on top of
him and pinned him underneath with his head turned to the side.
He had trouble breathing and found it impossible to dislodge the
heavy machine. Just when he thought he would die, the vehicle
was suddenly lifted off his body and placed back on solid ground,
upright and in a normal position. He never saw anybody, but he
knew it must have been an angel who had rescued him.

Jesus instructed His disciples: *"Truly I tell you, whatever you
bind on earth will be bound in heaven, and whatever you loose on earth
will be loosed in heaven"* (Matthew 18:18 NIV). What should we
loose on earth and in heaven? Angels! Under the Lord Jesus, this is
part of the authority of a believer. (See Revelation 9:14.).

When we loose God's angels, they surround us, helping to lift the heavy burdens that seem impossible for us to manage on our own.

ANGEL PRAYER

Everlasting heavenly Father, I seek for Your will and Your word of authority so that I can participate boldly in loosing angels. Every glimpse into heaven shows millions of angels ready to spring into action—some to guard and protect Your people, some to warn them, some to minister comfort and strength, and some to guide them in Your steps. I pray out of heartfelt love for my Savior, Jesus. Amen.

27

ANGELS ARE READY AND WILLING…ARE YOU?

God sent an angel to shut the lions' mouths.

My God sent his angel, and he shut the mouths of the lions. They have not hurt me, because I was found innocent in his sight. Nor have I ever done any wrong before you, Your Majesty."　　　　　　　　　　　(Daniel 6:22 NIV)

God could have come from heaven to shut the lions' mouths Himself, but He sent His angel instead. Angels are His ministering spirits (see Hebrews 1:14), and He sends them on all kinds of errands. His angels of protection are kept busy all the time—day and night.

Psalm 103:20 declares, *"Praise the LORD, you his angels, you mighty ones who do his bidding, who obey his word"* (NIV). Angels, like the servants of a mighty king, carry out their Master's decrees and declarations. They are attentive to God's Word and are quick to fulfill it.

You and I receive protection from angels more than we realize. We become involved in the process when we declare God's Word, standing, as we do, in the authority of redeemed followers of Christ Jesus. Could it be that angels of protection are waiting for you to speak with the voice of their King? The angels who are ready to *"obey his word"* and *"do his bidding"* are activated the moment they hear God's Word uttered through those of us who are the heirs of salvation. We are *"kings and priests to God and His Father"* (Revelation 1:6), and it is our responsibility to give voice to His Word.

I'll never forget the time that Janet and I were driving to Montreal, on our way to catch a plane to Purvirnituq, Nunavik, in the Canadian Arctic. The weather conditions were certainly not favorable for the long, eight-hour road-trip. Blizzard conditions caused whiteouts of snow on the frozen highway the entire length of our journey. In the middle of the night, about halfway to our destination, we hit a patch of slippery black ice that caused our vehicle to spin in circles. Without missing a beat, Janet immediately began speaking in her heavenly prayer language—not out of fear, but rather, in faith, knowing that her heavenly language would activate heavenly help on our behalf. It certainly worked. Although we never saw the visible hands of our angels, we could surely feel them placing our car directly into the middle lane, just as two large semi-trucks passed us on either side. Had we not been positioned in that exact way, we would've surely been struck and even possibly lost our lives. Speaking God's words brought God's angels immediately onto the scene.

We can be confident that angels will spring into action in accordance with the words of God. Right now, look up some verses that promise God's protection. Speak them out as a promise, and you can be confident of a supernatural level of protection for yourself.

There is no place too far, too high, too low, or too difficult for God's angels to reach you.

ANGEL PRAYER

A prayer from Psalm 20:6–9 (NIV): "Now this I know: the LORD gives victory to his anointed. He answers him from his heavenly sanctuary with the victorious power of his right hand. Some trust in chariots and some in horses, but we

> trust in the name of the LORD our God. They are brought to
> their knees and fall, but we rise up and stand firm. LORD....
> Answer us when we call!" Through Jesus, amen.

28

ANGELS UNVEIL THE MYSTERIES OF PROPHETIC VISION

The angel Gabriel was sent to Daniel to help him understand a vision from God.

> And I heard a man's voice between the banks of Ulai, which
> called, and said, Gabriel, make this man to understand the
> vision. (Daniel 8:16)

Just as the archangel Gabriel helped Daniel understand his overpowering vision from God, so angels are sent to individuals in this day to help them unwrap the mysteries of a prophetic vision. I know this from personal experience.

When I was in my early twenties, I had a dream in which I was taken up above the earth to encounter three of my guardian angels. They introduced themselves to me by name and explained to me the specifics of their ministry in my life. The first angel said his assignment was to release creative miracles, signs, and wonders wherever I ministered and to bring me unusual gifts and blessings from heaven. The second guardian angel was an angel of praise and worship. He said he would administrate the flow of heaven's sound and new songs throughout my life. The third angel explained that his assignment was to release holy boldness and strength when I was feeling weak and timid.

These revelations made sense to me because of some recent confirming occurrences involving all three of these areas. The concurring witness in my spirit was explosive.

I was amazed at the appearance of these enormous angels because they resembled me; they looked like my angelic brothers! They were wearing gleaming white robes and were much taller and broader than I am. Their hairstyles were distinctive and their eyes were swirls of heavenly colors, but I could identify them as my own angels.

After that I experience, I began to look for more information regarding angels and to position myself for further revelations. Over the years, the presence of angels—not limited to these three—has increased continually in my personal life and ministry life. Whenever I have needed new revelation, angels have brought it.

Not only can angels bring revelation, but they can also help recover any lost items that seems to have gone missing in your life, whether it is of a spiritual nature, an emotional need, or even some physical things that you've lost.

My friend Chlo is a pastor in London, England, and she recently shared a story with me about a remarkable time when she experienced the assistance of angels. Several years ago, she and her husband, Stu, went on the mission field to Kakamega, Kenya, where they were able to minister the gospel in several locations, including at a youth conference, during which they experienced such a torrential storm that they were forced to rush back to their accommodations. When it was time for them to pack up and head back to the airport, Chlo suddenly realized that she didn't have her Bible. They looked all around the room to find it, to no avail. This wasn't just an ordinary Bible. This was Chlo's most precious Bible, a priceless possession that had been given to her at her confirmation. It held all of her personal notes, as well as underlines and highlights of favorite Scriptures. How would she ever get it back? While trying to remember what had happened to it, Chlo had a vision in the spirit in which she saw that she had left it on a table at the front of the sanctuary where they had been preaching at the youth conference. In all the rush and chaos of the storm, she had left it behind. Now, back at the hotel, Chlo lifted her gaze toward heaven and prayed, "Father, You know how much this Bible means to me. You know how much revelation I've received from this book, the places it's been with me, and the tears I've shed over it. Father God, if You have any angels to spare right now that could do Your bidding on my behalf and fetch my Bible, I would be really blessed, because I don't want to leave this country without it." She continued praying, "Thank You, in Jesus's name, that my Bible is going to be returned to me now."

She opened her eyes and they went to pick up their bags to leave the room. Right there, on top of their luggage, was her precious Bible, in the very place they had already looked! Surely there was no other explanation for this miracle except for the ministry of angels.

ANGEL PRAYER

Heavenly Father, Lord of my life, open my spirit eyes and reveal the angels You have assigned to my life. I am willing and eager to meet them and to be better equipped to work together with them, as well as with Your Spirit. Help me to hide Your Word in my heart so I can more readily speak Your truth and engage their help. May Your holy name be ever more magnified through my life. Trusting in Jesus's name, amen.

29

VISIONS AND DREAMS

Gabriel appeared again to Daniel while he was in prayer.

While I was still in prayer, Gabriel, the man I had seen in the earlier vision, came to me in swift flight about the time of the evening sacrifice.   (Daniel 9:21 NIV)

Daniel's divine encounters took place largely in the context of visions and dreams. We often refer to "dreams and visions" in the same breath because both are ways of seeing into the supernatural world. (Dreams are visions that occur when a person is sleeping; visions are dreams we experience while awake.) Both ways of receiving revelation are highly personal, and only the person who is dreaming or seeing the vision can discern the image.

Many times, angels are the main players in a vision. Ezekiel encountered cherubim in his visions. (See Ezekiel 1, 10.) The apostle John recorded fifty-two visionary angelic encounters in the book of Revelation. Having first seen him in a vision, Daniel could recognize *"the man"* (the angel) Gabriel when he came again.

In our ministry meetings, I often become aware of angels in the room through what I call an "open-eye vision." My eyes are open and I can see the normal things around me, but the eyes of my spirit can see an overlaid image of angels—or whatever else the Lord wants to show me. Some people receive visions within their spirits. These are just as legitimate as open-eye visions. I would call them "impressions" or "knowings."

Once, when I was ministering at the Healing Rooms in Spokane, Washington, I saw a vision of an angel carrying what appeared to be a life jacket. In my spirit, I understood this to represent a new pair of lungs being delivered through the ministry of a healing angel, as lungs serve a lifesaving function. Later, a woman told me that those lungs had been for her. Apparently, just as I was announcing the angelic lung delivery, she could suddenly breathe more deeply than before. Prior to that moment, she had always felt short of breath and was unable to walk any distance without becoming winded. She believed she had been the recipient of those new lungs I saw in the vision.

ANGEL PRAYER

Open the eyes of my spirit to receive visions and dreams, heavenly Father. I want to see what is going on in the angelic realm, and I want to receive the blessings You have reserved for me. Educate me to understand Your heavenly communications and show me what to do with the visions and dreams You give me. Use me to share Your heavenly touch with the people around me. I love You and I love Your ways. Gratefully Yours, I ask this in the name of Your Son, Jesus. Amen.

30

YOU MAY BE LEFT SPEECHLESS

An angel came to Daniel in answer to his prayers.

I looked up and there before me was a man dressed in linen, with a belt of fine gold from Uphaz around his waist. His body was like topaz, his face like lightning, his eyes like flaming torches, his arms and legs like the gleam of burnished bronze, and his voice like the sound of a multitude.

I, Daniel, was the only one who saw the vision; those who were with me did not see it, but such terror overwhelmed them that they fled and hid themselves. So I was left alone, gazing at this great vision; I had no strength left, my face turned deathly pale and I was helpless. Then I heard him speaking, and as I listened to him, I fell into a deep sleep, my face to the ground.

A hand touched me and set me trembling on my hands and knees. He said, "Daniel, you who are highly esteemed, consider carefully the words I am about to speak to you, and stand up, for I have now been sent to you." And when he said this to me, I stood up trembling.

Then he continued, "Do not be afraid, Daniel. Since the first day that you set your mind to gain understanding and to humble yourself before your God, your words were heard, and I have come in response to them. But the prince of the Persian kingdom resisted me twenty-one days. Then Michael, one of the chief princes, came to help me, because I was detained there with the king of Persia. Now I have come to explain to you what will happen to your people in the future, for the vision concerns a time yet to come."

While he was saying this to me, I bowed with my face toward the ground and was speechless. Then one who looked like a man touched my lips, and I opened my mouth and began to speak. I said to the one standing before me, "I am overcome with anguish because of the vision, my lord, and I feel very weak. How can I, your servant, talk with you, my lord? My strength is gone and I can hardly breathe."

Again the one who looked like a man touched me and gave me strength. "Do not be afraid, you who are highly esteemed," he said. "Peace! Be strong now; be strong."

When he spoke to me, I was strengthened and said, "Speak, my lord, since you have given me strength."

So he said, "Do you know why I have come to you? Soon I will return to fight against the prince of Persia, and when I go, the prince of Greece will come; but first I will tell you what is written in the Book of Truth." (Daniel 10:5–21 NIV)

Daniel had been exiled to Babylon along with many other Jews and was looking for the fulfillment of prophetic words about their return to their native land. Not knowing what to expect, he fasted and prayed for three solid weeks. At the end of his epic prayer campaign, a powerful angel came to him. The other men in the room fled in terror. Only Daniel received the full revelation. And it nearly undid him.

But the angel strengthened him so that he could withstand the glory—and record the words that were spoken. He had been positioned for this.

ANGEL PRAYER

Father God, You are awesome beyond description, and Your angels come like flames of fire to scour the face of the earth. Without claiming as great a status as Daniel had, I nevertheless am willing to lay myself down in obedience. Position me, Lord, for the specific movements of Your Spirit that You want me to participate in, whether they are vast or minuscule. Your angels will provide the strength to fulfill Your commands. I pray in Jesus's name, amen.

31

GLORY BEYOND WORDS

Two angels brought revelation to Daniel.

> *Then I Daniel looked, and, behold, there stood other two, the one on this side of the bank of the river, and the other on that side of the bank of the river. And one said to the man clothed in linen, which was upon the waters of the river, How long shall it be to the end of these wonders? And I heard the man clothed in linen, which was upon the waters of the river, when he held up his right hand and his left hand to heaven, and swore by Him that lives for ever that it shall be for a time, times, and a half; and when He shall have accomplished to scatter the power of the holy people, all these things shall be finished.*
>
> (Daniel 12:5–7)

The *"other two"* and *"the man clothed in linen"* were angels. Unusual for angels, they delivered a long and detailed prophetic word to Daniel, the meaning of which had to remain a mystery, even though it had been spoken in plain words. Daniel strove to comprehend: *"And I heard, but I understood not: then said I, O my Lord, what shall be the end of these things?"* (verse 8).

The angel clothed in the linen garment lifted up his hand and said, *"Go your way, Daniel: for the words are closed up and sealed till the time of the end"* (verse 9). Then he continued, saying that the wicked of the earth would do still more evil before the word of God's deliverance came to pass, and that Daniel could not expect to penetrate the mystery of it all. *"Blessed is he that waits,"* said the angel (verse 12). *"But go you your way till the end be: for you shall rest, and stand in your lot at the end of the days"* (verse 13).

Even today, people disagree about what the angels' prophetic words mean. But the "wait and see" message is crystal clear. The angels' message was recorded for all time, and the effect of their delivery was powerful. A major spiritual shift took place as a result.

None of us can expect an angel encounter of the magnitude of Daniel's. But we can know what it's like to experience an almost tangible shift in the atmosphere, along with clues that angels have arrived.

Years ago, we started noticing rainbows appearing in unlikely places, even in the dark. Sometimes a rainbow would appear indoors. Even when we turned off the lights, the rainbows remained, even though, logically, there was no light present to be refracted into colors. Sometimes these were classic arched rainbows, but sometimes they appeared as a large streak of light, or like dancing colored lights all around a room.

How can rainbows appear in the dark? Well, God is light, and his angel messengers are filled with His glory light. Couldn't the rainbows be refractions of that light?

Today, I almost take it for granted that an unusual rainbow must be the calling card of an angel or two. A double rainbow is especially significant. Find all of the Bible verses that deal with a "double portion" blessing and pray into the Scriptures to find the message God is bringing to you through his angels! (See Deuteronomy 21:17; 1 Samuel 1:5; 2 Kings 2:9; Isaiah 61:7.) I have learned that such angelic visitations bring about a positive shift in the atmosphere, even (perhaps especially) in the darkest moments of my life. When I can tell that God has sent His angels to me, I don't mind being unable to understand everything.

ANGEL PRAYER

Lord, I invite You to bring me one of Your shifts right where I need it most. I welcome Your response to my request, regardless of the form it takes. Your ways are perfect all of the time, and I delight in the endless variety of manifestations of Your glory. Open my heart to receive every nuance, even if my mind is insufficient to appreciate the full meaning of Your advent.

32

ANGELS OF THE NATIONS

An angel brought revelation to Zechariah.

During the night I had a vision, and there before me was a man mounted on a red horse. He was standing among the myrtle trees in a ravine. Behind him were red, brown and white horses. I asked, "What are these, my lord?" The angel who was talking with me answered, "I will show you what they are." Then the man standing among the myrtle trees explained, "They are the ones the LORD has sent to go throughout the earth." And they reported to the angel of the LORD who was standing among the myrtle trees, "We have gone throughout the earth and found the whole world at rest and in peace." Then the angel of the LORD said, "LORD Almighty, how long will you withhold mercy from Jerusalem and from the towns of Judah, which you have been angry with these seventy years?" So the LORD spoke kind and comforting words to the angel who talked with me. Then the angel who was speaking to me said, "Proclaim this word: This is what the LORD Almighty says: 'I am very jealous for Jerusalem and Zion, and I am very angry with the nations that feel secure. I was only a little angry, but they went too far with the punishment.' Therefore this is what the LORD says: 'I will return to Jerusalem with mercy, and there my house will be rebuilt. And the measuring line will be stretched out over Jerusalem,' declares the LORD Almighty. Proclaim further: This is what

> the LORD Almighty says: 'My towns will again overflow with
> prosperity, and the LORD will again comfort Zion and choose
> Jerusalem.'" Then I looked up, and there before me were four
> horns. I asked the angel who was speaking to me, "What are
> these?" He answered me, "These are the horns that scattered
> Judah, Israel and Jerusalem."   (Zechariah 1:8–19 NIV)

God has many angels who have been designated to interact in
national and international affairs. In various meetings, intercessors have reported that they could see angels of the nations represented by the attendees and by the nations that are being prayed for. These angels watch and listen, waiting to hear the Scripture-based words that will be declared or decreed, which they hasten to bring to pass. When we faithfully speak out prayers and decrees that are based on the Word of God, He and His faithful angels move heaven and earth.

> This is what the LORD Almighty says: "In a little while I will
> once more shake the heavens and the earth, the sea and the
> dry land. I will shake all nations, and what is desired by all
> nations will come, and I will fill this house with glory.... The
> silver is mine and the gold is mine.... The glory of this present
> house will be greater than the glory of the former house....
> And in this place I will grant peace...."
>
> (Haggai 2:6–9 NIV)

ANGEL PRAYER

Heavenly Father, You are the Lord of everything, large and small, and I worship You. I have come to recognize and welcome the ministry of angels in my personal life, and now I also recognize and welcome the ministry of angels You have assigned to my nation and to other nations. Make me more sensitive to their activity so that I can pray for the accomplishment of Your purposes in their spheres of influence. In Jesus's name, amen.

33

RANK AND FILE

An angel gave Zechariah revelation concerning Jerusalem.

Then said I, Where go you? And he said to me, To measure Jerusalem, to see what is the breadth thereof, and what is the length thereof. And, behold, the angel that talked with me went forth, and another angel went out to meet him.

(Zechariah 2:2–3)

Almighty God never promises to do anything without a purpose, and I believe that He assigns special angels to help carry out every single one of His promises. Here with Zechariah, we see an angel whose assignment involves measurement and assessment joined by another angel who urges the first one to deliver a message: *"Run, speak to [Zechariah], saying, Jerusalem shall be inhabited as towns without walls for the multitude of men and cattle therein: for I, says the LORD, will be to her a wall of fire round about, and will be the glory in the midst of her"* (Zechariah 2:4–5). A long prophetic word ensues as Zechariah continues to engage with the angel and God pours out His heart toward Jerusalem's inhabitants.

To the present day, He assigns angels according to their rank and type. I have come to see that He has a number of ministering angels who could be categorized by their typical tasks: angels of joy, healing, prosperity, abundance, blessing, comfort, protection, and deliverance. The list goes on and on.

One of the angels I call "angel of divine love," must have been the kind of angel that helped Eliezer, Abraham's servant, to find a bride for his son Isaac: *"The LORD God of heaven…shall send His angel before you, and you shall take a wife to my son from there"* (Genesis 24:7). Eliezer would not be on his own as he went up and down the countryside looking for the perfect wife for Isaac.

If Zechariah, Abraham, and Eliezer were so conscious of the directed activities of angels on their behalf, how much more should you and I be, living in these days when the Spirit of God has been poured out upon all flesh. (See Acts 2:17.) Believe for the fulfillment of God's every word!

ANGEL PRAYER

Thank You, heavenly Father, for giving me a greater awareness of angels on assignment. I am grateful and in awe to think of the way Your angels watch over my personal and family life, as well as my church, city, and nation. I know they have been sent by You for Your purposes, and I trust You to help me understand why they have come and how I can better partner with them. Open lines of communication between heaven and earth! Praying in the name of Jesus, amen.

34

IF A DARK ANGEL VISITS

Zechariah had an encounter with an angel and with Satan himself.

Then he showed me Joshua the high priest standing before the angel of the LORD, and Satan standing at his right side to accuse him. The LORD said to Satan, "The LORD rebuke you, Satan! The LORD, who has chosen Jerusalem, rebuke you! Is not this man a burning stick snatched from the fire?"

Now Joshua was dressed in filthy clothes as he stood before the angel. The angel said to those who were standing before him, "Take off his filthy clothes." Then he said to Joshua, "See, I have taken away your sin, and I will put fine garments on you." Then I said, "Put a clean turban on his head." So they put a clean turban on his head and clothed him, while the angel of the LORD stood by. The angel of the LORD gave this charge to Joshua: "This is what the LORD Almighty says: 'If you will walk in obedience to me and keep my requirements, then you will govern my house and have charge of my courts, and I will give you a place among these standing here.'"

(Zechariah 3:1–7 NIV)

As we have just seen, angels played a prominent part in the prophet Zechariah's visions and prophecies. Most of the time, he saw and heard from the Lord's angels, but in this case, he also saw the fallen angel known as Satan. Satan and the other angels who fell with him cannot be trusted, and to this day, they fight against God's angels. Zechariah had a ringside seat to view the conflict.

Satan (also called Lucifer), and the angels who chose to follow him, are demonic angels of darkness who actively oppose the work of God's kingdom. (See Matthew 25:41; 2 Peter 2:4; Jude 1:6; Ephesians 6:12.) True angels of God's light are called "elect" (see 1 Timothy 5:21) or "holy" (see Matthew 25:31 and Mark 8:38), and they faithfully carry out God's will. We must learn to discern the difference.

Not that we need to cower in fear before Satan and his demons. In Jesus's name, we have full authority to cast them out. (See Mark

16:17; Luke 10:19.) Remember, only one-third of the angels in heaven fell with Lucifer. (See Isaiah 14:12; Luke 10:18; Revelation 12:4.) That leaves two-thirds who are true angels of light. Although Satan sometimes tries to disguise himself as *"an angel of light"* (2 Corinthians 11:14), we can learn how to spot him.

Sometimes, our discernment will be assisted by the presence of odors, both pleasant and unpleasant. When angels are present, people often report smelling pleasing and delightful aromas, such as roses (associated with Christ Himself) or the smoky aroma of a burning sacrifice. Sometimes, they feel the *"weight of glory"* (2 Corinthians 4:17). When demons are lurking, people sometimes detect foul odors, such as cigarette smoke or feces. It sometimes feels as if a big rubber band has been placed around my head with no warning, and by that unpleasant and even painful sensation, I know the devil is around. Others report a suffocating sensation.

If I sense the presence of darkness, I take authority over any evil spirits present, in Jesus's name, and cast them out, telling them where to go. Release occurs every time. Satan is not omnipresent or even slightly as powerful as God is. As a defeated enemy, he has been allowed to plague us for now. Let's not allow ourselves to fall for his accusations.

ANGEL PRAYER

You are the One I love and serve, Father in heaven. I want nothing to do with the enemy. I pray that You will increase my discernment so that I can tell whether I am sensing angels of light or not. Defend me as I go about on Your assignments, and equip me with all the weapons of spiritual warfare that I need. My heart is steadfast, and I want to keep it that way. In the name of Your Son, Jesus, amen.

35

AWAKENED BY AN ANGEL

Zechariah next encountered an angel who instructed him.

And the angel that talked with me came again, and waked me, as a man who is wakened out of his sleep, and said to me, What see you? And I said, I have looked, and behold a candlestick all of gold, with a bowl upon the top of it, and its seven lamps thereon, and seven pipes to the seven lamps, which are upon the top thereof: and two olive trees by it, one

*upon the right side of the bowl, and the other upon the left side
thereof. So I answered and spoke to the angel that talked with
me, saying, What are these, my lord? Then the angel that
talked with me answered and said to me, Know you not what
these be? And I said, No, my lord.*   (Zechariah 4:1–5)

Zechariah never stopped learning. His prophetic gift was amazing, and so was his humility. In this story, the angel initiated the communication; he did not wait for Zechariah to open his mouth with questions. When the angel spoke to him, Zechariah entered into a real conversation with him. Until the angel instructed him, he did not understand the meaning of what he was seeing.

Zechariah had learned that the unseen supernatural realm was more real than the earthly realm where he ate and slept. It was as though he had read the words the apostle Paul wrote centuries later: *"So we fix our eyes not on what is seen, but on what is unseen, since what is seen is temporary, but what is unseen is eternal"* (2 Corinthians 4:18 NIV). You and I need to be convinced of this truth: the unseen realm is the most real realm.

It is often the case that angels are present, and yet, unseen. Through the eyes of our spirits and our other spiritual senses, we can discern them. Angels can appear so frequently that we assume they are merely strangers. Other times, they appear as bright light (see Luke 2:9), light that does not cast a shadow (see James 1:17), as clothed in cloud formations (see Daniel 7:13; Psalm 104:3), or as shadows (see Psalm 63:7). Often enough, they signal their presence with heavenly aromas.

With many others, I have known the reality of an angel's touch. While remaining invisible, angels may stroke your hair or place their hands reassuringly on your back or shoulder.

Not too long ago, my wife, Janet, and I were staying at a hotel in Calgary, Canada, preparing to teach an Angel School, in which we activate and engage the students in angelic interactions. Little did we realize that we would have an encounter of our own before we even got to the school! At about five o'clock in the morning, Janet felt a tapping at her feet. She tried to roll over and ignore it but the intense tapping continued. When she arose, she realized that an angel had been tapping her feet because he was trying to get her attention. You see, we have a new puppy named Buttercup and she needs to eat breakfast every morning at seven. Janet had given our son Lincoln some instructions to feed her at this time. But, clearly, the angel knew it wasn't happening, so he flew cross-country, across two time zones, in order to wake up Janet so that she would call Lincoln and ask him to feed our puppy! Isn't that amazing? You might think that's just a silly little story but I want you to know that God really cares about every area of your life. He has angels watching out for you, and angels ready to wake you up if you need it!

If something like that happens to you, remember that the unseen realm is the most real realm, much more real than the chair you are sitting on!

ANGEL PRAYER

Heavenly Father, send Your Holy Spirit to enliven my spirit to discern the presence of angels. It is too easy for me to dwell in this material realm and to ignore the signs of Your unseen realm. I am still learning the language of heaven, and I pray that You will speak to me in ways that are clear and simple. It's wonderful to discover an angel in the room. Keep sending them and keep teaching me more. In Jesus's name, amen.

36

ANGELS TAKE ON MANY DIFFERENT APPEARANCES

An angel came to help Zechariah understand a revelation from God.

Then the angel who was speaking to me came forward and said to me, "Look up and see what is appearing." I asked, "What is it?" He replied, "It is a basket." And he added, "This is the iniquity of the people throughout the land." Then the cover of lead was raised, and there in the basket sat a

woman! He said, "This is wickedness," and he pushed her
back into the basket and pushed its lead cover down on it.
Then I looked up—and there before me were two women,
with the wind in their wings! They had wings like those of a
stork, and they lifted up the basket between heaven and earth.
"Where are they taking the basket?" I asked the angel who
was speaking to me.　　　　　(Zechariah 5:5–10 NIV)

The angel replied that they were taking the basket back to
Babylon, which is where the idolatry of materialism (represented
by the woman in the basket) had originated.

Zechariah was in the midst of a series of graphic visions, inter-
preted for him by an angel. In some of the visions, other angels
appeared. In this one, it is possible that the *"two women"* who *"had*
wings like those of a stork" were angels.

Angels are spirit beings who can choose to manifest in any
physical form. They are not limited to one body, as we are. They
can appear as either male or female—or neither. (See Matthew
22:30.) Sometimes they look like animals. (See Ezekiel 1:10.)
They can appear in terrestrial or atmospheric conditions, such as
storms, fire, rainbows, clouds, and earthquakes. (See, for example,
2 Kings 6:17; Ezekiel 1:4; Matthew 28:2; Luke 20:36.)

In Palm Springs, California, where our ministry is based,
there is a natural phenomenon that occurs during the early morning hours on the lower slopes of the San Jacinto Mountains. To the
careful observer, a shadow can be seen taking on the form of a large
angel with outspread wings, which seems to rise on the mountainside, overlooking the entire valley below. There are many local leg-
ends about this mysterious formation but it is known locally as "The

Angel on the Mountain." Tourists rise early to take photos of it, and for those who catch a glimpse of it experience great joy and peace, as we are reminded that angels *do* watch over our valley at all times.

Now, I'm not saying that the shadow is an actual angel. It isn't; it's only a reminder. You see, our world is filled with various visible reminders in the natural that remind us of what we don't always see in the supernatural. The Bible says, *"The heavens declare the glory of God; and the firmament shows His handiwork. Day to day utters speech, and night to night shows knowledge. There is no speech nor language, where their voice is not heard"* (Psalm 19:1–3).

Sometimes people see butterflies appearing around them, repetitively, almost as though God is trying to get their attention through this occurrence. The same thing often happens with hummingbirds or other winged creatures, reminding us of God's holy angels, with glory in their wings. These creatures are not angels, only reminders. Other people look into the sky and notice interesting cloud formations. Their minds are captivated as they see images of horses dancing through the sky or enormous angels with swords drawn. Again, these are reminders. Not everyone may see them, or if they do, they may not feel the same way about them that you do because it is your personal reminder.

God loves to speak to you in a very personal way. Some people have told me that they are reminded of God's angels whenever they see the pure, sparkling snowflake falling through the air. Others have seen shapes and images of angels in the frozen ice formations left on winter window panes. Several years ago, a church in Tennessee noticed beautiful angelic images filled with colored light appearing in the windows of their sanctuary. Many people came to see them and were deeply touched. Again, such visible displays vary, but they all are personal reminders to you. Let us remember that angels never appear to bring glory to themselves. They do not want to be worshipped. The angels in your life desire to point you toward the life-giving presence of Jesus Christ. All goodness comes from Him.

ANGEL PRAYER

Father in heaven, continue to manifest Your presence here on earth in every way, and make me aware of Your presence so that I can fully cooperate with what You are doing. I give You glory for what You have done in the past and what You will do in the future. I praise You especially for tapping me to be part of Your team, along with Your angels. Keep me close at all times. I rest in You and I pray in Jesus's name. Amen.

37

TALKING WITH ANGELS

Again, an angel came to help Zechariah understand a revelation from God.

Then I answered and said to the angel that talked with me, What are these, my lord? And the angel answered and said

to me, These are the four spirits of the heavens, which go forth
from standing before the Lord of all the earth.

(Zechariah 6:4–5)

It is okay to ask angels questions. In this case, Zechariah had
seen a vision of "*four chariots coming out from between two moun-*
tains—mountains of bronze. The first chariot had red horses, the
second black, the third white, and the fourth dappled—all of them
powerful" (Zechariah 6:1–3 NIV). Zechariah had no idea what
they represented.

The angel not only explained that they represented "*the four*
spirits of the heavens," but that they were issuing forth from the
Lord's presence to travel in different directions to punish nations.
The chariots symbolize war and carnage, and the colors of the
horses carried prophetic importance.

My point here is not to expound on the prophetic details,
but rather to emphasize how readily angels will reply to a person's queries. You can ask angels to explain revelations. You are
not expected to understand everything on your own. If angels are
present with you in the moment, it is part of their job description
to help you understand what you are seeing. When you understand better, then you can get on with your part in the fulfillment
of God's will.

In addition, your prayers open the way for angelic activity. As
you intercede and communicate with God, you open the airwaves
between heaven and earth. Angels are activated to move upon the
highway of your prayers.

Throughout Scripture, we see this in operation. Daniel's prayers released a mighty angel to explain a crushing vision. The angel spoke of the role his prayers had played: *"Do not be afraid, Daniel. Since the first day that you set your mind to gain understanding and to humble yourself before your God, your words were heard, and I have come in response to them"* (Daniel 10:12 NIV). The early church learned how to press into the Spirit through prayer in order to activate the angelic realm. This is what happened in the story of Peter's release from prison in Acts 12:5–11. The church prayed. Angels responded.

You must receive an anointing of the Spirit to pray in this way. In addition to meshing with God's plan in the strength of the Spirit, your Spirit-led prayers will open your eyes to the supernatural realities of angels around you. Just remember, the way angels come to help us is often much different from what we may expect or imagine. That's why it is so important to keep your heart open when you pray to God. He always listens and your prayers always release angels, but you must learn to see the way in which God responds, and trust the answer He brings when it comes. Your attitude will determine what you see.

ANGEL PRAYER

Heavenly Father, I am beginning to understand Your supernatural cause and effect. I seek Your face and pray the prayers You lay on my heart. I keep praying persistently, if that's what seems to be required. Then You give me eyes to see the results—and they often involve angelic activity. Help me overcome my natural reticence in the face of such powerful experiences. If I need to understand Your revelatory messages, I want to ask questions in the moment. I will need Your help every time. I ask this in Jesus's name. Amen.

38

THE DOORWAY TO THE SUPERNATURAL

The angel Gabriel announced to Mary that she had been chosen to be the earthly mother of Jesus.

In the sixth month the angel Gabriel was sent from God to a city of Galilee, named Nazareth, to a virgin espoused to a man whose name was Joseph, of the house of David; and the virgin's name was Mary. And the angel came in to her, and said, Hail, you that are highly favored, the Lord is with you: blessed are you among women. And when she saw him, she was troubled at his saying, and cast in her mind what manner of salutation this should be. And the angel said to her, Fear not, Mary: for you have found favor with God. And, behold, you shall conceive in your womb, and bring forth a son, and shall call His name JESUS. He shall be great, and shall be called the Son of the Highest: and the Lord God shall give to Him the throne of His father David: and He shall reign over the house

of Jacob for ever; and of His kingdom there shall be no end.
Then said Mary to the angel, How shall this be, seeing I know
not a man? And the angel answered and said to her, The Holy
Ghost shall come upon you, and the power of the Highest shall
overshadow you: therefore also that holy thing which shall be
born of you shall be called the Son of God. And, behold, your
cousin Elisabeth, she has also conceived a son in her old age:
and this is the sixth month with her, who was called barren. For
with God nothing shall be impossible. And Mary said, Behold
the handmaid of the Lord; be it to me according to your word.
And the angel departed from her.   (Luke 1:26–38)

The doorway to the supernatural realm is in your heart, not your head. Remember, Jesus lives in your heart, not in your brain. Mary could not wrap her mind around the angel's prophetic message; such a thing seemed to be utterly impossible. But in her spirit (her heart), she was willing to believe it.

No one before or since has been given the same word as Mary's word from Gabriel. But every word from God, whether big or small, whether delivered through an angel or not, must be received through the human spirit. God's Spirit speaks to our spiritual hearts. We "hear" with the ears of our spirit and "see" with the eyes of our heart. After the angel visited Mary, Scripture goes on to say, "*Mary kept all these things, and pondered them in her heart*" (Luke 2:19). She didn't meditate on them in her mind, she reflected on them in her heart.

The apostle Paul wrote, "*I pray that the eyes of your heart may be enlightened in order that you may know the hope to which he has called you, the riches of his glorious inheritance in his holy people*"

(Ephesians 1:18 NIV). Notice, Paul did not pray for our natural eyes and ears to see and hear God's message. He knew better.

I often ask God to open my "spirit eyes and ears," even when I am also paying attention with my natural eyes and ears. It's like tuning in my personal radio receiver to receive invisible signals from heaven.

ANGEL PRAYER

Heavenly Father, I ask for Your Spirit to open the eyes of my heart that I might become more aware. By Your Spirit, help my spirit to discern Your words to me. I desire to see and hear Your angels so that I can receive Your messages through them. I open my heart to receive this gift of spiritual awareness. In Jesus's name, amen.

39

ANGELS WHO BRING RELIEF FROM DEEP CONCERN

In a dream, an angel encouraged Joseph to take Mary as his wife.

But while he thought on these things, behold, the angel of the Lord appeared to him in a dream, saying, Joseph, you son of

David, fear not to take to you Mary your wife: for that which
is conceived in her is of the Holy Ghost. (Matthew 1:20)

Joseph was dismayed. His young Mary was pregnant by some other man? She had seemed so unlikely to transgress the simple terms of their betrothal pledge. It was all he could think about. What should he do? As a man of honor, he didn't want to put her to shame, but if she now belonged to another man, he would not be able to take her as his wife. After a long day filled with troubled thoughts, Joseph lay down to sleep.

Sometime during the night, he began to dream, and an angel stood before him, speaking to his deep concerns. *"Joseph, you son of David, fear not to take to you Mary your wife: for that which is conceived in her is of the Holy Ghost."* The angel continued, *"And she shall bring forth a son, and you shall call His name JESUS: for He shall save His people from their sins"* (verse 21).

This must be true! Wide awake, he waited until dawn to go to Mary's house and make it official, taking her home with him as his wife.

It was almost as important for Joseph to go along with God's plan as it was for Mary to say "yes"—and how could either of them have assented to such unlikely pronouncements without the visible and audible involvement of angels?

None of us can ever expect to have the same need of reassurance and direction that Mary and Joseph did, but several times in my life, I have felt the touch of angels of comfort. They did not speak. Each time, I was troubled by a difficult situation, and as I committed the details to the Lord, I felt a gentle, affirming hand resting on my shoulder or touching my back. Have you ever felt anything like that?

ANGEL PRAYER

Heavenly Father, most of the time, I have no trouble believing that You are watching over my life to protect me from mishaps or mistakes. But I know I can find it almost impossible to lay hold of the simple trust I want to live by when I'm dealing with a troubling or tumultuous situation. In those times, I thank You for sending me angelic reassurance. I need help from heaven in order to keep trusting You with my whole heart. Thank You for Your perfect encouragement. Because of Jesus's perfect sacrifice, amen.

40

AWESOME HEAVENLY ENCOUNTERS

Gabriel notified elderly Zechariah that he and his barren wife would become the parents of John the Baptist.

There was in the days of Herod, the king of Judaea, a certain priest named Zechariah, of the course of Abia: and his wife

*was of the daughters of Aaron, and her name was Elisabeth.
And they were both righteous before God, walking in all the
commandments and ordinances of the Lord blameless. And
they had no child, because that Elisabeth was barren, and they
both were now well stricken in years. And it came to pass, that
while he executed the priest's office before God in the order of
his course. According to the custom of the priest's office, his lot
was to burn incense when he went into the temple of the Lord.
And the whole multitude of the people were praying outside
at the time of incense. And there appeared to him an angel
of the Lord standing on the right side of the altar of incense.
And when Zechariah saw him, he was troubled, and fear fell
upon him. But the angel said to him, Fear not, Zechariah:
for your prayer is heard; and your wife Elisabeth shall bear
you a son, and you shall call his name John. And you shall
have joy and gladness; and many shall rejoice at his birth.
For he shall be great in the sight of the Lord, and shall drink
neither wine nor strong drink; and he shall be filled with the
Holy Ghost, even from his mother's womb. And many of the
children of Israel shall he turn to the Lord their God. And he
shall go before Him in the spirit and power of Elijah, to turn
the hearts of the fathers to the children, and the disobedient to
the wisdom of the just; to make ready a people prepared for
the Lord. And Zechariah said to the angel, Whereby shall I
know this? for I am an old man, and my wife well stricken
in years. And the angel answering said to him, I am Gabriel,
that stand in the presence of God; and am sent to speak to
you, and to show you these glad tidings. And, behold, you
shall be dumb, and not able to speak, until the day that these*

things shall be performed, because you believe not my words,
which shall be fulfilled in their season. (Luke 1:5–20)

When the angel Gabriel appeared to him next to the altar, Zechariah was stricken with a mixture of reverence, respect, fear, and amazed wonder.

I'm sure that Mary and Joseph also felt a similar awe during their arresting angelic encounters, but there is a significant difference between their responses (immediate, courageous obedience) and Zechariah's reaction (incredulity).

We often lightly say, "I don't believe it!" when something out of the ordinary occurs; but in Zechariah's case, his unbelieving response brought memorable consequences: he would not be able to utter a word until the promised baby boy was born. He suffered his punishment of silence patiently, and everything worked out as the angel had said. His initial misgivings gave way to firm belief after all.

Centuries earlier, Zechariah's forefather Jacob had been awestruck when he saw angels moving up and down a ladder to and from heaven. He enthused, *"How awesome is this place! This is none other than the house of God; this is the gate of heaven"* (Genesis 28:17 NIV). That's the response God is looking for when angels appear. He wants to see your awe- and faith-filled response.

Not long ago, I found out that my friend Pam was hosting a monthly Bible study at her home in San Diego, California. This thrilled my heart because I've known Pam for more than twenty years and her hunger for God has only ever increased. I told her, "Pam, I'm coming to your Bible study. I want to be a part of it."

She replied, "You know it's just in my house, right?"

I said, "Yes, I know! That's why I want to come!"

God does good things when spiritually hungry people gather together.

A few weeks later, I found myself at Pam's home. She had rearranged the living room and dining room furniture so that the maximum amount of people could gather in her home. We began to worship together and within minutes, the presence of God's glory came upon us in a tangible way. Immediately, in the atmosphere of God's presence, it was obvious that angels were moving to and fro around the house. Like waves crashing over us, various heavenly aromas were being poured out. Some people smelled roses; others smelled lilies. It was as though we were walking through the garden of the Lord in our worship. Many miraculous things happened that night as people were caught up into visions and felt the healing touch of God. One moment in glory changes everything.

Angels can comfort us by bringing beautiful aromas, singing heavenly songs, or playing supernatural music in our atmosphere. Everything they do comes with the presence of heaven and draws us closer to the love of God.

One fun thing you can do with your Bible study group, or at home with some close friends, is read aloud some of the stories from this book. See these testimonies as supernatural doorways for you to access new spheres in God. After you read a chapter or two, discuss your feelings and what you sense the Lord saying. Begin to pray into it and see God releasing something new for you.

ANGEL PRAYER

What can I say, Lord? I am so in awe of You, even though I have yet to see the myriads of angels that dwell in Your heavens. I have seen something of Your glory through Your angels, and I want to see more while I still inhabit this body on earth. May I find new ways to express my complete faith in You as my all-loving Father and saving Lord. Because of You, Father, Son, and Holy Spirit, amen!

41

PAY ATTENTION TO ANGEL WARNINGS

An angel warned Joseph to take Mary and Jesus and flee to Egypt.

Behold, the angel of the Lord appeared to Joseph in a dream, saying, Arise, and take the young Child and His mother, and flee into Egypt, and be you there until I bring you word: for Herod will seek the young Child to destroy Him.

(Matthew 2:13)

King Herod was greatly disturbed when he learned that a baby who would claim the title "King of the Jews" was purported to have been born in Bethlehem. His only thought was that this rival king must be eradicated before He could grow up and make trouble! Herod enlisted the Magi to scout out the scene in Bethlehem, and when they purposely failed to bring back a report, he determined to act anyway. Stooping to a new low in wickedness, he decided to have all of the baby boys in Bethlehem killed. (See Matthew 2:16.)

But by the time Herod's orders were carried out, the Child was no longer there, because Joseph had been warned by an angel to take his little family and flee to faraway Egypt, beyond the reach of the murderous king. This is one of the clearest examples in Scripture of an angel delivering a warning.

What can we learn from this? One essential truth is that no angelic warning does any good if the one warned does not take it seriously and follow through, as Joseph did. The angel's words did not do away with Joseph's personal responsibility to undertake a challenging journey into the unknown. That was Joseph's part, and the angel could not do it for him.

When Peter was challenged by the tax collectors as to whether or not his master, Jesus, paid His taxes, Peter asked Jesus about it. Jesus told him to go fishing: *"So that we may not cause offense, go to the lake and throw out your line. Take the first fish you catch; open its mouth and you will find a four-drachma coin. Take it and give it to them for my tax and yours"* (Matthew 17:27 NIV). Peter nodded and went to fetch his fishing line. Everything happened exactly as Jesus had said. (Who put the coin there? I surmise that it was an angel.) The mission was simple but highly unusual. Peter's quick compliance with Jesus's instructions made the miracle possible.

There have been several occasions in my life in which angels have been involved in warning me about the direction I was heading. For example, a few years ago, I was driving from the airport back to my home. Although there are two different ways I can travel, I have a favorite route that I like to take. As I was about to continue on that route, I suddenly heard a voice speak to me from the passenger seat, although I was traveling all alone in the car. The voice said, "Go the other way." I didn't question it. Without hesitation, I took the alternative route. Later, I discovered that there had been a serious accident along my normal route. Would I have been in an accident had I not listened to the voice that spoke? Quite possibly. At other times, the warnings have come like subtle nudges in my spirit. Whether these nudges are the voice of the Holy Spirit or an angel reaching out to warn me doesn't matter. I'm thankful that God shows concern for us and desires for us to be protected wherever we go.

When we take a directive from God seriously and act on it, we make a connection between the supernatural and natural world. We become much more efficient and effective in fulfilling our life mission. Everything we do in obedience to God becomes a seed for a future harvest. Sometimes, it may mean the difference between life and death!

ANGEL PRAYER

Father, I confess that I have dropped the ball a few times. I am sure that You have tipped me off more than once, and I have shrugged off the warnings or instructions. Even when You have sent an angel to speak to me, I have decided that the words were too outrageous to obey. Please give me another chance. I offer myself to You once again as an obedient servant/son and I turn my heart to follow You. Make me quick to obey, like Joseph. Humbly, because Jesus lives, amen.

42

GUARDIAN ANGELS: OUR EARTHLY COMPANIONS

An angel told Joseph when it was safe to return home.

But when Herod was dead, behold, an angel of the Lord appeared in a dream to Joseph in Egypt, saying, Arise, and take the young Child and His mother, and go into the land of Israel:

for they are dead which sought the young Child's life."
(Matthew 2:19–20)

Just as angels deliver warnings and strategies for victory, so also do they issue the "all clear" when a dangerous time has passed. Much of the time, I believe this task falls to our personal guardian angels.

Some people think guardian angels are a childish concept, but I do not. For example, I read the words of the Psalms: *"The angel of the LORD encamps around those who fear him, and he delivers them"* (Psalm 34:7 NIV), and *"He will command his angels concerning you to guard you in all your ways; they will lift you up in their hands, so that you will not strike your foot against a stone"* (Psalm 91:11–12 NIV). I call the angels who have been assigned as our personal spiritual and physical protectors, "guardian angels." Jesus referred to such angels: *"See that you do not despise one of these little ones. For I tell you that their angels in heaven always see the face of my Father in heaven"* (Matthew 18:10 NIV).

It has been said, "A guardian angel walks with us, sent from above; their loving wings surround us and enfold us with God's love." Sometimes, your guardian angel may appear to have wings, while other angels do not. Some people have seen their guardian angels towering over them, ten or twenty feet tall, while others have noticed that their angels appear to be vertically challenged. The size of your angel is never to be a concern. They are spiritual beings and they all carry great power and ability.

I would go so far as to say that guardian angels may well look like the person to whom they have been assigned. At least mine seem to be. When people tell me they can see an angel with me, they often add, "And the angel looks just like you." I wonder if that is the reason the gathered believers mistook Peter's surprise appearance at their door for an angel instead. (See Acts 12:6–15.)

I believe that our guardian angels care about every detail of our lives. No concern is too great or too small for them. Recently, a dear friend reached out to me with a puzzling question that had been troubling he: "I do believe in angels and the fact that God gives them charge over us, but where was my guardian angel when I was mugged coming home from church on Easter Sunday a few years ago?"

This question took me by surprise, so I went to prayer and I asked the Lord about it. God told me, "Joshua, I have given everybody a free will. I am not able to force anybody to do something against their will. Bad things happen because people choose to go against *My will*. But this is not My desire. My angels surround the lives of My children to help guide them and guard them against the attacks of the enemy. I deliver messages through My angels that help to protect My children, but even if those messages are not heeded, I have still ordained that My children will defeat the attacks of the enemy. My angels will help My children overcome."

Through this revelation, I understood this to mean that there were limits to what guardian angels could and could not do. Here are my conclusions:

+ Guardian angels often "nudge us" away from unknown dangers and evil intentions. We will never know how often this has happened in our lives.

- If we don't follow the promptings from our guardian angels, God will still attempt to speak to others in order to get the message through. He is always watching out for our good.

- Guardian angels cannot force a person to do or stop doing anything. This includes ceasing the abuse of another person. Angels do not "wrestle against flesh or blood." It is a spiritual battle. Evil intentions come from the enemy and are empowered by the sinful nature.

- When evil things happen, which is always against the will of God, God's plans for His children are still good. (See Jeremiah 29:11.) Your guardian angels have been directed by God to help you to turn around any situation that has brought you loss or tragedy, or made you to feel like a victim. That's why Psalm 91:12 says, *"In their hands they shall bear you up"* (NKJV).

Stacey shared a testimony about her encounter with an angel. She said that the angel of the Lord appeared to her but she didn't initially heed the call. Even after the angel visibly made himself known and reached out to her, she still went her own way, down the path of destruction. But the angel continued to pursue her with God's loving kindness and, eventually, her heart was softened to receive God's love and salvation. You see, God can't and won't force anybody to love him, but He will pursue you with His goodness until you come to your senses and realize that His way is the best way.

ANGEL PRAYER

Heavenly Father, there is so much joy in the journey of life because of the company of angels. They keep me safe from perils, and I so rarely recognize their protective hand. I thank You for setting things up so that each one of us can trust in Your perfect provision. Make me more aware of it so I can raise my voice with new praises. Worshipping You because of Jesus, amen.

43

SUPERNATURAL SUDDENLIES

An angel appeared to Judean shepherds, announcing the birth of the Christ Child.

And there were in the same country shepherds abiding in the field, keeping watch over their flock by night. And, lo, the angel of the Lord came upon them, and the glory of the Lord shone round about them: and they were sore afraid. And the angel said to them, Fear not: for, behold, I bring you good tidings of great joy, which shall be to all people. For to you is born this day in the city of David a Savior, which is Christ the Lord. And this shall be a sign to you; you shall find the babe wrapped in swaddling clothes, lying in a manger. And suddenly there was with the angel a multitude of the heavenly host praising God, and saying, Glory to God in the highest, and on earth peace, good will toward men.   (Luke 2:8–14)

One moment, the shepherds and their flocks were cloaked in starlit darkness, with only the muffled sleepy sounds of the animals; the next moment, the whole sky lit up. The shepherds were used to watching for the threats of predators that lurked in the darkness, but they had never, ever, seen or heard the likes of this! I'm sure it was much more dramatic and glorious than all of the electronic special effects a movie director might bring to the scene today.

"*Suddenly*" is a key word. The angel appeared that way to Peter in prison, too. "*Suddenly an angel of the Lord appeared and a light shone in the cell*" (Acts 12:7 NIV). Peter certainly was not expecting that. The church's prayers for Peter had been going up for some time, but when the answer came, it was sudden.

One of my friends used to be a stunt actress in Hollywood and she told me about a time when she seriously injured herself on a movie set. Just as the paramedics were preparing to take her away by ambulance, a little girl who appeared to be about nine years old *suddenly* came out of nowhere, running toward her to give her a hug. When my friend saw this precious girl's face, she was taken aback, because this beautiful little girl looked exactly like her! It was oddly amazing. The girl said that she wanted to pray for my friend, and as she did, she prayed out loud with bold faith. Later that day, my friend was taken to the hospital where she was bandaged up and able to recover. But the amazing thing about this story is that the directors and producer went to look for that young girl but she was nowhere to be found. Could it be that God sent an angel to minister in the right place, at just the right time? I think so.

In our time of hurt, God knows exactly what we need. If you're hurting right now, God has a host of heavenly angels ready to come and minister to you. You may not see them with your natural eyes, but that's okay. Just close your eyes and sense their presence around you. Sense these angels laying their hands upon you, releasing healing and peace that removes all pain and discomfort.

Angels bring God's "suddenlies," and I like to think they enjoy doing it.

ANGEL PRAYER

Heavenly Father, Son, and Holy Spirit, send forth Your glorious angels to shatter the darkness around me. Bring to my mind Your promises and Your words of truth, and show me how to prepare my heart to react with obedient joy. I am looking forward to this! In Jesus's name, amen.

44

EVEN JESUS NEEDED ANGELS

Angels ministered comfort to Jesus after His encounter with Satan.

Then the devil leaves Him, and, behold, angels came and ministered to Him.   (Matthew 4:11)

Even Jesus needed the ministry of angels. After withstanding the temptations of Satan in the wilderness for forty days, He was depleted beyond human remedy. Angels came to restore His strength. Later, when He was praying in the garden of Gethsemane in preparation for His crucifixion, He was overwhelmed by the crushing burden of His impending sacrifice. He had brought His trusted disciples to watch with Him, but they fell asleep under a tree. Only angels could help Him, and they did.

Notably, they did not swoop down to extricate Him from the situation, although that could have happened. In fact, He scolded His disciples when one of them tried to defend Him from arrest, saying, *"Do you think I cannot call on my Father, and he will at once put at my disposal more than twelve legions of angels? But how then would the Scriptures be fulfilled that say it must happen in this way?"* (Matthew 26:53–54 NIV).

The angels fortified Him so that He could fulfill His Father's will. And so they will fortify us as we face our lesser but still daunting challenges. Jesus taught that we, His disciples, would do the same things He did, and even *"greater works than these"* (John 14:12). This means that we will be able to shoulder our assignments from God with full confidence of angelic assistance. We should not be surprised when angels arrive in force. In fact, we can request it. God has not promised us a problem-free existence. In fact, hardships are guaranteed. But He has promised to help us, and His angels do His bidding.

Janet and I spent a month with a team of others in New Zealand, ministering in many places. While we experienced the tangible presence of God in every single meeting, we were expending a lot of energy and grew weary. We had completed only about half of our scheduled meetings, and the constant travel and demanding pace were taking their toll.

One night, we returned to our hotel room to find that angels had brought us something to strengthen us—golden leaves from heavenly trees! We were astonished. Here were delicate leaves made of gold, placed upon the open pages of one of our Bibles. One of the team members received a revelation about them: these leaves were meant to be eaten, like the supernatural food the angels provided for Elijah. (See 1 Kings 19:5–7.)

Thus, we ate the miraculous golden leaves, and they brought strength and wholeness to our weary bodies. In fact, because of our newfound strength, we were able to take a rigorous day trip the next day, trekking as a team to the top of Mount Rangitoto. And for the rest of the month, we continued to minister in the supernatural strength that had been imparted in such an unusual way.

ANGEL PRAYER

Oh, Father in heaven, there is no end to Your provision and care! You take care of impossible situations and help Your children to press forward in supernatural strength. Increase my expectation for more. I want to overcome my natural reluctance to expect angelic assistance. I know You will send the right help at just the right moment. I am holding out my empty hands with faith and joy. Expectantly, in Jesus's name, amen.

45

SOME ANGELS BRING STRENGTH

An angel appeared to Jesus in the garden of Gethsemane to strengthen Him.

And there appeared an angel to Him from heaven, strengthening Him.   (Luke 22:43)

Almost perishing in the face of His overwhelming anguish, the Son of God needed supernatural strength to go through with the agony of His arrest, flogging, and execution. Later, on the cross, He would feel abandoned. But here in the garden, His Father sent an angel to shore Him up.

None of us will ever have to face such agony, but we do need angelic help and strength to alleviate our stress and strengthen us to be faithful to our commitments. In the face of unexpected disruptions or emergencies, we need much more help than we can get by phoning 9-1-1.

That's when we need to call on our angels. Unlike us, they never get stressed out or afraid. They never even get tired. You will feel a calming presence when God's angels minister strength to you. Your symptoms of anxiety will dissipate. You will be able to think clearly. You will be enabled to carry on despite extreme physical discomfort. You will feel the touch of heaven.

When she was younger, our daughter, Liberty, almost died. A sudden, severe illness required her to be placed on life support in the hospital. Janet and I took turns sitting with her around the clock as she lay sedated in her bed. Even though we were praying for her healing—which did come eventually—the ordeal of waiting in the face of a dire diagnosis was wearing us out.

One night, Janet was with her, praying. The lights were low and the nurses came in intermittently to check Liberty's vital signs. In the wee hours of the morning, Janet sensed a shift. She began to feel a light, cooling wind as well as the presence of God's glory. It strengthened her, both physically and spiritually. Healing angels had entered the room.

At that moment, some nurses pulled aside the curtain and stopped abruptly. As they went back and forth, they kept commenting on what they were feeling—a "special peace" in Liberty's room. For the rest of the night, Janet could feel the strengthening peace of the angels' presence, and she told the nurses where it was coming from.

That was the night Liberty turned the corner. Seventeen days after she was put on life support, she returned home with a clean bill of health. We praise God for His complete healing—and for giving us strength and freedom from fear as we waited.

ANGEL PRAYER

Heavenly Father, I believe these words: *"He shall give His angels charge over you, to keep you in all your ways"* (Psalm 91:11). I believe that You have assigned at least two angels to watch over my steps, to strengthen me in the face of daunting challenges, and to minister Your comfort to me. I know I take this for granted most of the time. If I close my eyes and take a deep breath, I can picture two large angels on either side of me. I know that they watch over me, day and night, tirelessly. Thank You for this amazing provision! You leave nothing to chance, and I praise You for Your fatherly care, especially in sending Your Son Jesus, in whose name I pray. Amen.

46

IS IT NORMAL TO FEEL AFRAID OF ANGELS?

The angel at Jesus's tomb reassured the women.

> *In the end of the sabbath, as it began to dawn toward the*
> *first day of the week, came Mary Magdalene and the other*
> *Mary to see the sepulcher. And, behold, there was a great*
> *earthquake: for the angel of the Lord descended from heaven,*
> *and came and rolled back the stone from the door, and sat*
> *upon it. His countenance was like lightning, and his raiment*
> *white as snow: and for fear of him the keepers did shake, and*
> *became as dead men. And the angel answered and said to the*
> *women, Fear not you: for I know that you seek Jesus, which*
> *was crucified.*
> (Matthew 28:1–5)

Fear is a common reaction to supernatural encounters. But have you noticed how many times in Scripture the same angel who caused the fear speaks reassuringly, saying "fear not!" and then goes on to deliver a message that helps to explain his appearance? Even Daniel, whose supernatural experiences were greater than ours, needed reassurance: *"Then* [the angel] *continued, 'Do not be afraid, Daniel. Since the first day that you set your mind to gain under-standing and to humble yourself before your God, your words were heard, and I have come in response to them'"* (Daniel 10:12 NIV).

We do not have to feel ashamed of such fear. It is normal to be alarmed by overpowering majesty. Our life experience has trained us to be apprehensive when confronted suddenly by something that is unfamiliar or unexplained. But we need to take an angel's reassurance to heart so we can move forward into whatever God is doing. Remember Paul's words to Timothy: *"For God has not given us the spirit of fear; but of power, and of love, and of a sound mind"* (2 Timothy 1:7).

When I was a child, I suffered from occasional episodes of sudden, paralyzing fear. This overwhelming fear came in response to an evil presence; dark angels (evil spirits) were trying to short-circuit my destiny as one who would minister with God's angels. This was far more than childish fear of monsters under the bed (although I think we should pray for our kids when they have such fears instead of dismissing their distress as foolishness). We need to plant their feet (and our own) firmly on the truth that God's angels surround them at all times, protecting them from all harm.

Fear not, He protects you from evil!

ANGEL PRAYER

Heavenly Father, I am Your child and I trust You as my Father. I commit myself to Your care. Banish insecurity, anxiety, and panic, and convert my remaining fears to faith. Help me to secure a healthy, awe-filled fear of Your glorious presence. I want to dwell under the protective wings of Your angels and know that You are with me at all times. Because of Jesus, amen.

47

ANGELS OF HARVEST

Two angels instructed Jesus's disciples when He ascended to heaven.

> *And while they looked steadfastly toward heaven as He went up, behold, two men stood by them in white apparel; which also said, You men of Galilee, why stand you gazing up into heaven? this same Jesus, which is taken up from you into heaven, shall so come in like manner as you have seen Him go into heaven.* (Acts 1:10–11)

Why did angels appear just as Jesus disappeared into the sky? These ministering angels were sent to explain what had just happened, and to help keep the disciples on track. Jesus was leaving them on their own to spread the radical new gospel message, and He knew they would need supernatural assistance. It wouldn't be easy, but He had just told them what to expect: *"It is not for you to know the times or the seasons, which the Father has put in His own power. But you shall receive power, after that the Holy Ghost is come upon you: and you shall be witnesses to Me both in Jerusalem, and in all Judaea, and in Samaria, and to the uttermost part of the earth"* (Acts 1:7–9).

Matthew's version captures His words this way, which we call the Great Commission: *"All power is given to Me in heaven and in earth. Go you therefore, and teach all nations, baptizing them in the name of the Father, and of the Son, and of the Holy Ghost: teaching them to observe all things whatsoever I have commanded you: and, lo, I am with you always, even to the end of the world"* (Matthew 28:18–20).

How on earth would these early believers be capable of witnessing to the uttermost parts of the earth? Only with the ever-present help of the Holy Spirit—who would often make His presence known through those special ministering spirits, the angels of harvest.

Angels of harvest, some of whom reap the harvest on their own and some of whom assist believers in the task, are the ones that John the Revelator wrote about in Revelation 14:15.

As disciples, we have been commissioned by Jesus to go into the whole earth, proclaiming the good news, reaping a rich harvest from every nation. This would be an impossible assignment without supernatural help. Where are you with all of this? Are you following through? Are you leaning on the Holy Spirit?

I've had the privilege of traveling to spread the gospel in more than seventy-five nations around the world. And there's one thing I can tell you for sure: I have never gone alone. Yes, the Holy Spirit resides inside of me, so He goes with me everywhere that I go. But He has also ordered His angels to follow me and work with me in this great reaping of the nations. The first time I went to minister in Bangkok, Thailand, the auditorium was packed to capacity. The hunger for the things of God was so great that, because of their excitement, many people were taking photos during the meetings. It soon became apparent in almost every photo that I was surrounded by hosts of angels all around me. Images of light appeared behind me, beside me, above me, and below me. This amazed the people that were capturing the photos, but it is something that has become quite common for me. Angels of harvest are always working with me as I go to the nations. As another confirmation of their presence, the altars were packed later that night with many people making first-time decisions for Christ.

Are you willing to learn how to work with angels of harvest? They are willing to work with you!

ANGEL PRAYER

Heavenly Father, I am thinking of a situation right now that I believe You want to address. You want to reach out through me to bring someone into Your kingdom. I have run into a brick wall before in similar situations, but this time, I ask You to empower me in a new way. Holy Spirit, clear the approach path and soften hearts. Angels of harvest, stand ready with your sickles! Jesus, bind us together under Your lordship in a new and successful effort. Amen.

48

ANGELS ON DUTY

An angel freed the apostles from prison and told them what to do in response to persecution.

> *Then the high priest and all his associates, who were members of the party of the Sadducees, were filled with jealousy. They arrested the apostles and put them in the public jail. But during the night an angel of the Lord opened the doors of the jail and brought them out. "Go, stand in the temple courts," he said, "and tell the people all about this new life."*
>
> (Acts 5:17–20 NIV)

Angelic interventions are not limited only to apostles or other "important" people. Every single believer has angels who have been commissioned to perform certain tasks on his or her behalf. Many of them provide protection and deliverance from harm, while others deliver timely messages.

"The angel of the LORD encamps around those who fear him, and he delivers them" (Psalm 34:7 NIV). This means that specific angels have been assigned to *you*. This is true whether or not you ever acknowledge their existence.

Thanks to one of those on-duty angels, the apostles spent only half a night in jail, and could return immediately to their assignment of preaching the gospel. This angel also told them what to do next, and it wasn't, "Run away and hide in a safe place!" Angels would continue to guard their steps, even in an environment of severe persecution.

Both the Old and New Testaments document a full range of angel activity. As we explore these stories and become aware of the comprehensive applications of their assistance, we must also come to see that every example represents an area of our own lives in which angels can work. We learn that angelic intervention doesn't always involve thrilling escapades. More often, our Shepherd is simply taking care of our welfare.

For instance, via angels, He brings us into a new life of joy. Actually, angels are much more attracted to joy than to any other emotion because it's more than an emotion—it's an atmosphere. The Bible says that God sits in the heavens and laughs! (See Psalm 2:4.) Wherever great joy abounds, you can be sure that there are also a great number of angels.

Many years ago, I met a minister named Darrel, who told me that angels didn't like most church services because the music was too slow and boring. He said, "Angels like fast, upbeat, praise music! They love it when people are dancing!" I wasn't quite sure how he knew this until later on in the service, when turned to the congregation and said, "Take out your cameras and begin taking pictures in here." Then he instructed the audio technician to play a recording of an upbeat, joyful song. As the music played, he instructed people to begin dancing and having fun in God's presence. It was fun, for sure, and many people received breakthroughs in their praise, but when the song was finished, he addressed the crowd once again, saying, "Now, take out your cameras and capture photos in the sanctuary again." He explained that before we praised, there will be no signs of any angels in your photos, but after we praised and sang and danced before the Lord, the place filled with angels. "Just look at your photos," he proclaimed. To everyone's amazement, it was true! Many people captured digital photos of angels filling the atmosphere all around us! It was amazing. You should try this experiment sometime too! Joy seems to be a magnetic attraction for angels.

Since all angels originate from the presence of God, the atmosphere of joy feels like home to them. Remember, the Bible says that "in the presence of the Lord, there is joy forevermore." (See Psalm 16:11.) One of the tasks that angels carry out is bringing this atmosphere of joy to people in various situations, no matter how bleak things may look in the natural. One sure sign that an angel is present and ministering is a feeling of joy in the Lord rising up inside of you, even when you are facing a difficult circumstance or you are experiencing a devastating blow in your life. This joy comes from the Lord, but it is most frequently delivered into our lives through the ministry of angels. Through angelic ministry, many people have been delivered from depression, others have been restored after suffering traumatic abuse, and countless lives have been refreshed—all because angels bring *"good tidings of great joy, which shall be to all people"* (Luke 2:10)!

ANGEL PRAYER

Thank You for Your unfailing care, Father above. You want what is best for me and You teach me how to trust in Your provision. It's wonderful to know that You have assigned angels to me, and that they are on duty, 24/7, never running out of energy or taking a vacation. I put You first in my life, today and every day, because of the love of Your Son, Jesus. Allow me to radiate Your love wherever I go. I ask in Jesus's name. Amen.

49

DIVINE GPS (GOD'S POSITIONING SYSTEM)

An angel brought directions to Philip.

> *The angel of the Lord spoke to Philip, saying, Arise, and go toward the south to the way that goes down from Jerusalem to Gaza, which is desert.* (Acts 8:26)

Philip had just completed an exciting stretch of ministry in Samaria and had returned to Jerusalem with the other apostles. Suddenly, an angel instructed him to travel down the desert road that connected Jerusalem to Gaza. He dropped everything and went.

Philip was finely tuned to God's word of direction, wasn't he? That's why God could accomplish His purposes in a straightforward manner. The angel didn't tell him *why* he was supposed to go to the desert road, just that he was to *"arise, and go,"* and Philip complied with the instructions without hesitation. I believe that if God sends His word to someone who proves to be unwilling to comply, the angel must go looking for someone who is more willing. In this case, he didn't have to.

On the road, Philip encountered an Ethiopian eunuch, and the rest is history. He led the man into God's kingdom without missing a beat. Then, God's Spirit transported him miraculously, and he found himself at Azotus, many miles further west and north, without having to trek there on foot. How's that for a day's work? Once he complied with the angel's initial words of direction, a series of miracles could occur. (See Acts 8:27–40.)

Angels have many different ways in which they can communicate with us and help to bring God's directions for any given situation. Many years ago, while we were ministering near Rockford, Illinois, a lady came to our meetings with a jar full of dimes. She explained that for many months she had been collecting them wherever she went. She found them on the sidewalk as she walked down the street; she found them on a bench at the local shopping mall; some appeared inside the hymnal at church; when she drove her car, she would notice them resting on the dashboard; she even found some inside her refrigerator freezer! None of it made sense to her, but she felt as though it was a supernatural sign of some sort. Dumbfounded by this experience, she asked us, "Do you know what this means?"

We had never heard about such a thing before, so we went to the Lord in prayer and He told us that His angels were trying to get her attention! Well, get her attention they certainly did, but she still didn't understand the message. The Lord further spoke to us and told us to research the number ten (the value of a dime), and all of its biblically significant meanings. This is what we found:

‣ The number ten is a biblically perfect and complete number. The Passover Lamb was chosen on the tenth day of the first month. This also correlates with the testimony of Jesus, who we know was the perfect sacrifice who came to take away the sins of the world. (See Exodus 12:3; John 12:28–29; 1 Corinthians 5:7.) In other words, the number ten tells us that everything has come full-circle and is in divine order.

‣ The number ten also represents responsibility. (See Exodus 20.) Moses was given the Ten Commandments, which now persuade us to repent and live a life empowered by the grace and glory of God. (See Exodus 24:7; Psalm 84:11.)

‣ The number ten is also an example of faith in God. (See Genesis 14:20, 28:20–22; Leviticus 27:30–32; Nehemiah 10:37–38; Malachi 3:8–10.) Through the tithe (giving God 10 percent of our income), we see the people of God bringing honor as they put their stewardship priorities into proper perspective.

So, as you can see, the message delivered by the angels to the women with the dimes was complex and deep. It needed to be decoded, but once it was, it became obvious! The clear directions were: "You have completed your past season. Let go of the past! God is bringing everything into divine order. Don't worry about the future. Your responsibility is to move forward by grace into the glory of God as you continue to walk by faith. Angels are watching over you to help you transition into your new season with ease." This message brought such freedom and joy to that woman, knowing that she was headed in the right direction and that she had God's angels watching over her to help!

Thank God for His angels and the unusual directions that they bring. Don't be surprised if you begin finding dimes now too. Pick them up and receive the message that is coming through!

ANGEL PRAYER

God in heaven, You are beyond good, and You never cease to amaze us with all that You do. How perfect Your ways are, and how carefully You are willing to guide us into them. Thank You for Your supernatural surprises. I ask You to release more of them into my life through the ministry assignments of Your angels. Ever grateful, I belong to You because of Jesus. Amen.

50

MANIFESTING ABUNDANCE WITH THE ANGELS

An angel told Cornelius to summon Peter to tell him about God.

He saw in a vision evidently about the ninth hour of the day an angel of God coming in to him, and saying to him, Cornelius. And when he looked on him, he was afraid, and

*said, What is it, Lord? And he said to him, Your prayers and
your alms are come up for a memorial before God.... And
Cornelius said, Four days ago I was fasting until this hour;
and at the ninth hour I prayed in my house, and, behold, a
man stood before me in bright clothing, and said, Cornelius,
your prayer is heard, and your alms are had in remembrance
in the sight of God. Send therefore to Joppa, and call here
Simon, whose surname is Peter; he is lodged in the house of
one Simon a tanner by the sea side: who, when he comes, shall
speak to you.*   (Acts 10:3–4, 30–32)

Why was the angel sent to this particular non-Jewish Roman military officer? According to the story, it was because of Cornelius's generous giving. He contributed regularly to the needs of the poor, and he always prayed to God. His prayerful giving had risen like incense to the throne of God and God was rewarding him.

This illustrates a principle: generous giving, along with worship and directed prayers, serve as invitations to God, and He sends off angels in response. If you ask for God's direction regarding your financial and material stewardship, He will show you where you can sow your "seeds." And as you give in joyful obedience, God will release angels carrying rich blessings.

For Cornelius, the blessing that came as a result of his generosity of heart was salvation for himself and for his entire Gentile household. For us, the blessing often comes in spiritual, emotional, and even financial ways. It is not unusual in our meetings for "miracle money" to appear supernaturally in pockets, wallets, and purses, along with substantial financial breakthroughs in situations of need. Receiving such abundant provision time and again myself always makes me even more joyful, prayerful, and generous.

A man named Brian wrote me several years ago, thanking me for the revelation I had shared through one of my books about angels of prosperity. Until that day, he had never realized that these angels even existed, not to mention that they were ready and available to work in his life. He told me that this revelation had come at just the right time because, being a small business owner, his business had suffered during an economic downturn and it seemed as though the end was inevitable. Brian had been faithful in bringing his tithes to his local church, but he hadn't realized that it was possible to sow into the glory, or that angels of prosperity would use his seed to bring an accelerated harvest.

Although his finances were tight, Brian decided to sow a sacrificial seed into our ministry. As he did so, he decreed, "I know that angels of prosperity are moving on this seed. They are bringing an abundant harvest to me!" In his letter, he explained that at that time, several bills were coming due and it didn't seem as though there was any natural way to stretch the money that he had in his bank account. Wanting to be faithful to his commitments, he decided to write the first check to his landlord for the rent. As he wrote it, he made another decree: "I know that angels of prosperity are moving on my seed. They are bringing an abundant harvest to me!"

After a week, he noticed that the money he had written checks for hadn't come out of his bank account. Worried that the check may have been lost, he called his landlord, who seemed confused, and said, "I received your check and deposited it immediately. Your rent is paid." Bewildered, Brian checked his bank account again and, to his surprise, the finances were still there—no withdrawal had been made—and yet, his bill was paid. This seemed very unusual. Brian decided to write the next check to pay his electricity bill. As he wrote it, he decreed, "I know that angels of prosperity are moving on my seed. They are bringing an abundant harvest to me!" He sent his payment in the mail and, once again, the money never left his account, yet when he called the electric company about it, they said, "Sir, we received two months payment from you. You now have a credit balance and don't owe us any money!" Brian reported that the same thing happened for every one of his bills. They either were paid off unexplainably or double-paid to create a credit in his account. This financial miracle allowed him to get his business back in the black. He reported, "I know that these angels of prosperity are real! I asked for help, and I got it!"

Now this testimony might seem strange to you, but it's certainly not strange for the angels of prosperity. They are constantly available and willing to work with anybody who desires to trust God in the area of their finances. How did Brian's bills get paid? I'm not sure, exactly, but the angels know where an abundance of finance can be found, and they also know how to put it into the right places at the right times when people get their hearts right with God. Notice that Brian didn't allow fear to block his seed, but, instead, he overcame the spirit of poverty with a seed of faith!

After finishing a mid-week meeting in Los Angeles, we received an exciting report about angels of prosperity moving on behalf of a ministry couple in attendance. They told us, "We sowed five hundred dollars into the glory, and one hour later, someone donated five thousand dollars to us—ten times the amount we sowed! Later that night, when we went to bed, I had an encounter with two finance angels who walked right into our bedroom and stayed for an hour! They told me about their role and function in our lives and since that time, people have been sowing into our ministry like crazy!"

This is so exciting. These angels go by many and various names, including "Angels of Prosperity," "Angels of Finance," "Miracle Money Angels," and "Angels of Provision," but one thing true of all of them—these angels of abundance know how to connect you with unstoppable blessing and they are available to work for you today!

ANGEL PRAYER

Heavenly Father, Giver of all gifts, I pray that You would mold my heart to be like Yours—generous and loving. May I find the specific ways You want me to give of my time and money, and may I have Your Spirit's help to pray consistently in accordance with Your will. May my eyes of faith be opened to see Your blessings in whatever form they may take. With expectant faith, in Jesus's name, amen.

51

FREEDOM FROM CAPTIVITY

An angel released Peter from prison.

> *And, behold, the angel of the Lord came upon him, and a light shined in the prison: and he smote Peter on the side, and raised him up, saying, Arise up quickly. And his chains fell off from his hands. And the angel said to him, Gird yourself, and bind on your sandals. And so he did. And he says to him, Cast your garment about you, and follow me. And he went out, and followed him; and knew not that it was true which was done by the angel; but thought he saw a vision. When they were past the first and the second ward, they came to the iron gate that leads to the city; which opened to them of its own accord: and they went out, and passed on through one street; and immediately the angel departed from him. And when Peter was come to himself, he said, Now I know of a surety, that the Lord has sent His angel, and has delivered me out of the hand of Herod, and from all the expectation of the people of the Jews.* (Acts 12:7–11)

There are all kinds of prisons. The bars and chains that are holding you in captivity may be internal fears or circumstantial constraints. Are you facing a "prison" right now? Whenever you find yourself in bondage, helpless to set yourself free from a difficult and harmful situation, pray to the Father for deliverance.

When the angel came to Peter in his prison cell in response to the prayers of the church (see Acts 12:5), he was asleep and chained between two soldiers. At first, it must have seemed like a dream; it's not every day that an angel strikes you in the ribs and walks you past every guard and gate to freedom.

You would think that Peter would have been both terrified and ecstatic, but he remained the calmest person in the story. This has been my experience most of the time whenever angels appear to me. Even in the presence of the biggest and most fearsome angels, I never feel afraid or unduly emotional. Instead, I experience God's peace. I find it comforting to see an angel.

Not too long ago, I was facing a personal dilemma in my life and felt rather discouraged, not knowing quite how to handle the situation I was facing. In the natural, it seemed like a daunting ordeal and I really needed some help from heaven to help me navigate this problem. A few days later, an angel appeared to me in a dream one night. He was wearing a shimmering white robe and had a large golden belt around his waist, just like angels I had seen many times before. His face was filled with pure love and God's light, but what I noticed most about this angel was the marble tablet he held in his hand. On the tablet was a scriptural inscription. It was clear to me that God had sent this heavenly messenger to give me this specific and personal message. I felt the peace of God. When I awoke, I remembered exactly what I had seen, especially the Scripture that stood out clearly on the tablet in the angel's hands. I rushed to open the pages of my Bible and when I found the Scripture, it almost popped right up out of the Word! It was so clear! It was so obvious! It was God's answer to my present-day problem! I decided to do exactly what the Scripture instructed me to do. When I followed those God-given instructions, I supernaturally found the solution to my dilemma!

Expect God to send His angels to set you free! He wants you to be able to carry on with His assignments for you. *"For He shall give His angels charge over you, to keep you in all your ways"* (Psalm 91:11).

ANGEL PRAYER

Heavenly Father, Your Word declares that You will fortify and rescue me from the evil one, and that You will rescue me from all of my troubles. Here and now, I thank You for releasing Your angels of deliverance into my life. I rest in Your strength and faithfulness, trusting You for each moment. In the victory won by Your Son, Jesus, amen.

52

ANGELS REVEALING STRATEGIES

An angel assured Paul of safety during a storm at sea.

Paul stood forth in the midst of them, and said, Sirs, you should have hearkened to me, and not have loosed from Crete, and to have gained this harm and loss. And now I exhort you to be of good cheer: for there shall be no loss of any man's life among you, but of the ship. For there stood by me this night the angel of God, whose I am, and whom I serve, saying, Fear not, Paul; you must be brought before Caesar: and, lo, God has given you all them that sail with you. Wherefore, sirs, be of good cheer: for I believe God, that it shall be even as it was told me.   (Acts 27:21–25)

Paul was a prisoner. He was being taken to Italy by ship when it was caught in a terrible storm. The sailors were desperate. Surely they were all going to drown. How could this prisoner be so cheerful? Paul explained: *"There stood by me this night the angel of God, whose I am, and whom I serve, saying, Fear not, Paul; you must be brought before Caesar: and, lo, God has given you all them that sail with you. Wherefore, sirs, be of good cheer: for I believe God, that it shall be even as it was told me"* (Acts 27:23–25). It happened exactly as the angel had said.

Today, God is still showing people what to say by sending revelation through His angels. I think of one time when I was walking down Hollywood Boulevard with a friend. We noticed some activity and filming going on ahead of us on the street, and we stopped to watch. We didn't recognize any of the participants, but soon a woman stepped up behind us and began to fill us in. In particular, she named one celebrity and told us that he was a very popular singer in Asia. She went on to quietly reveal private details about his personal difficulties. It seemed inappropriate for someone to be sharing such information with strangers on the street. When our attention was drawn to the performance again, the lady disappeared into the crowd.

Later that same day, we decided to eat dinner at a steakhouse in Beverly Hills. Not twenty minutes after we had been seated, that famous singer was seated at the very next table. This was a divine set-up! We offered to pray for him and he agreed. We were able to lay hands on him—and we already knew exactly what to pray for. Not until later did we realize that the woman on Hollywood Boulevard must have been an angel.

About twelve months later, I was ministering in South Korea. Suddenly, that same celebrity singer appeared on the hotel television screen. He was sharing his testimony about how Jesus had saved him and then led him to establish one of the largest Christian youth ministries in Asia. Amazing!

ANGEL PRAYER

Heavenly Father, I give You first place in my life, and I want You to draw me into Your kingdom strategies. Help me grow in my awareness of the angelic messengers You send my way to help me understand what I can do. May Your kingdom come and Your will be done, in and through my life. In the mighty name of Jesus, amen!

EPILOGUE

I pray that as you've read through the biblical encounters in this book, you have been able to find yourself within the pages of God's Word. Every place where God allowed an angel to come and minister in the pages of Scripture represents an area of your life where God has an angelic encounter waiting for you. As you take time to focus and put into practice the things I've shared here, I believe you will experience an increase in the glory realm of God. Let the Holy Spirit bring transformation in your life as you surrender to His glorious presence.

In closing, please pray with me:

Heavenly Father, thank You for introducing me to these realms of angelic encounter. I receive every inspired word and revelation from heaven, and I invite Your angels to come and minister to me in the ways that You desire them to. Guide me in fully embracing everything You have for me, as I continue to fix my eyes upon You. In the precious name of Jesus, amen.

I believe God has already begun, and will continue, to work in your life, opening new doors in the glory for encountering your angels. I would love to hear your personal testimonies as you begin to encounter angels in your own life.

Please feel free to share them with me by email:
info@joshuamills.com

God bless and keep you!

ABOUT THE AUTHOR

Joshua Mills is an internationally recognized ordained minister of the gospel, as well as a recording artist, keynote conference speaker, and author of more than twenty books and spiritual training manuals. His recent books include *Moving in Glory Realms* and *Seeing Angels*. He is well known for his unique insights into the glory realm, prophetic sound, and the supernatural atmosphere that he carries. For more than twenty years, he has helped people discover the life-shifting truth of salvation, healing, and deliverance for spirit, soul and body. Joshua and his wife, Janet, cofounded International Glory Ministries, and have ministered on six continents in over seventy-five nations around the world. Featured in several film documentaries and print articles, including *Charisma* and *Worship Leader Magazine*, together, they have ministered to millions around the world through radio, television, and online webcasts, including appearances on TBN, Daystar, GodTV, *It's Supernatural! with Sid Roth*, *100 Huntley Street*, and *Everlasting Love* with Patricia King. Their ministry is located in both Palm Springs, California, and London, Ontario, Canada, where they live with their three children: Lincoln, Liberty, and Legacy.

www.JoshuaMills.com